CONTENTS

Author: **Theresa K. Buskey, B.A., J.D.**

Editor: Alan Christopherson, M.S.

Alpha Omega Publications

Published by Alpha Omega Publications, Inc.
300 North McKemy Avenue, Chandler, Arizona 85226-2618

THE CONTEMPORARY WORLD

The contemporary world is the world in which we live. Presenting current events in historical terms is a challenge. It is a challenge because this history is still being made. This LIFEPAC will present events from World War II until the present day. You will see how our world has been shaped by these events. You will be studying events your parents and grandparents lived. This is where history comes home. This is where the stream of life that you have studied all year reaches out and touches you.

In the first section you will study the **Cold War** between the United States and the Soviet Union. You will see how the developing conflict shaped post-war Europe. You will learn how the vast power and nuclear arsenals of the two super-powers kept them from fighting a direct war. You will study the crises and local wars that marked the conflict between them. You will learn how the conflict ended with the fall of the Soviet Union.

In the second section you will study the geography and current political status of the nations of the world. In a continent by continent survey you will see how the world has changed during the Cold War and how it has remained the same.

OBJECTIVES

Read these objectives. The objectives tell you what you will be able to do when you have successfully completed this LIFEPAC.

When you have finished this LIFEPAC, you should be able:

1. Describe the nature of the Cold War.

2. Name the major events of the Cold War.

3. Understand the basic structure of the United Nations.

4. Describe the course of the Korean and Vietnam Wars.

5. Describe the fall of communism in Eastern Europe and the collapse of the Soviet Union.

6. Describe the basic geography of the six inhabited continents.

7. Name the major mountains, rivers, lakes, and deserts of the six inhabited continents.

8. Recognize the names and locations of the countries of the world.

9. Have a basic understanding of the current status of the nations of the world.

Survey the LIFEPAC. Ask yourself some questions about this study. Write your questions here.

_____

_____

_____

_____

_____

_____

_____

_____

_____

THE COLD WAR

Introduction. The Cold War is the name given to the period that began at the end of World War II and ended with the collapse of Soviet power. During this time the two **superpowers**, The United States and the Soviet Union, did not fight an actual "hot" war with each other. Instead this war was fought in a series of confrontations and local wars throughout the world. The end of this period is so recent that it is not yet clearly defined. This LIFEPAC dates the end of the Cold War in 1991 when communism ended in the Soviet Union and the country was divided into new countries. Another possible date would be 1989, when communism collapsed in Eastern Europe and the **Berlin Wall** was dismantled. In either case, the Cold War ended with a victory for the United States.

SECTION OBJECTIVES

Read these objectives to learn what you should be able to do when you have completed this section.

1. Describe the nature of the Cold War.
2. Name the major events of the Cold War.
3. Understand the basic structure of the United Nations.
4. Describe the course of the Korean and Vietnam Wars.
5. Describe the fall of communism in Eastern Europe and the collapse of the Soviet Union.

VOCABULARY

Study these words and phrases to enhance your learning success in this section.

Cold War	satellites	Iron Curtain
containment	NATO	Warsaw Pact
thermonuclear	Intercontinental ballistic missiles	Demilitarized Zone
repatriation	superpowers	endemic
nominally	draft	Berlin Wall
purge	autonomy	

Note: All vocabulary words and phrases in this LIFEPAC appear in **boldface** print the first time they are used. If you are unsure of the meaning when you are reading, look the it up in a dictionary or encyclopedia.

ORIGINS OF THE COLD WAR

Post War Situation. The United States and the Union of Soviet Socialist Republics (U.S.S.R.) were the most powerful nations in the world at the end of World War II. Europe was devastated. Germany and Japan were in ruins from Allied bombing. The Soviet Union had a huge, well supplied army holding all of Eastern Europe and one third of Germany. The United States expected a period of friendly relations with the Soviet Union at the end of the war. After all, the two peoples had fought and died opposing a common enemy for four years. The U.S. expected to be able to use its influence during this time to convince the Soviet Union to withdraw from Europe peacefully. In fact, Joseph Stalin, the Soviet dictator, had no intention of allowing Eastern Europe to be free and possibly allied with the West.

Stalin acted quickly to secure his position, ignoring the promises he had made during the war. Estonia, Latvia, and Lithuania (the Baltic Republics) were annexed again (they had been taken in 1940 under an agreement with Hitler). Some Polish land was also taken by the Soviet Union. Poland was then compensated with a part of Soviet occupied Germany (this basically shifted the entire country west). The Allied leaders had actually agreed to this travesty at Yalta, an Allied conference during the war. Stalin had given in exchange "his word" that Poland and the other nations would be allowed to have free elections. Instead, pro-Soviet communist governments were set up in Poland, Hungary, Romania, Bulgaria, and Czechoslovakia. Yugoslavia and Albania set up communist governments of their own. These nations became Soviet **satellites** and were completely cut off from their free neighbors. In

1946, England's famous wartime leader, Winston Churchill, spoke of an **"iron curtain"** which now separated Europe into two opposing camps.

The United States immediately faced this new threat to the recently freed nations of Europe. When a communist take over was threatened in Greece in 1947, President Harry Truman chose to act. He realized that a return to the longstanding U.S. policy of isolation would leave the world unable to protect itself from Soviet aggression. He, therefore, formulated and announced the policy of **containment**, also known as the Truman Doctrine. This policy committed the United States to restrict communism to the places it already existed. Any attempt to spread it to new countries would be opposed by the United States throughout the world. In the case of Greece, $400 million in aid was sent to both Greece and Turkey which successfully defeated the communist rebels in their lands. Containment was to continue as the basic policy of the United States through all of the Cold War.

✳ Answer the following.

1.1   What are the two historical events, including dates, that could be used to mark the end of the Cold War.

a. _____

_____

b. _____

_____

1.2   Describe the policy of containment.

_____

_____

_____

1.3   Who were the primary antagonists during the Cold War?

a. _____

b. _____

1.4   The Soviet Union set up communist governments in:

a. _____   d. _____

b. _____   e. _____

c. _____

1.5   How did the United States expect to get the Soviets out of Eastern Europe after the war?

_____

_____

_____

1.6   What two nations set up their own communist governments after World War II?

a. _____

b. _____

United Nations. One ray of hope in the early years of the Cold War was the United Nations (UN). This international body had been formed in 1945 while the war was still being fought. Unlike its predecessor, the post-World War I League of Nations, the United Nations had the backing of the United States. The Soviet Union also joined. However, the United States and the Soviet Union both had a veto over any resolution passed by the organization. The Soviets used this freely to prevent any interference in their interests. Moreover, the UN had no enforcement power to back its decisions. It provided a forum for discussion and occasional action that were used by both sides in the Cold War.

The United Nations was created at a conference in San Francisco. Fifty nations signed the original charter that went into effect on October 24, 1945. The UN then accepted an invitation to set up its headquarters in the United States at New York City. The United Nations has six main organizational structures:

The General Assembly. All member states are represented in the General Assembly. The General Assembly makes all of its decisions by a majority vote, occasionally a 2/3 majority. Each country has one vote. The Assembly takes part in the election of the members for the other UN organizations. Its resolutions are not binding on any member nation except as they relate to the United Nations budget.

The Security Council. The Security Council is the UN organization responsible for keeping peace in the world. It consists of fifteen members, five of which (France, Great Britain, the United States, China, and Russia) are permanent members. The permanent members have a veto over any decision made by the council, otherwise decisions are made by majority vote. The Council can investigate and make recommendations on any matter it feels threatens world peace.

The Secretariat. The Secretariat consists of the secretary-general of the United Nations and his staff. The secretary-general is appointed by the General Assembly after being nominated by the Security Council. He serves a five year term. The Secretariat runs the day to day operations of the UN. The secretary-general is also able to use the prestige of his position to encourage solutions of international problems.

International Court of Justice. The Court of Justice is the judicial branch of the United Nations. Its fifteen judges are appointed to nine year terms. The court sits at The Hague, Netherlands. It gives advisory opinions to other UN branches and decides disputes between any governments that agree to submit a problem to the court. Decisions are by a majority vote of the judges.

The Economic and Social Council. The Economic Council is responsible for implementing United Nations projects to improve life on this planet. It works to improve health, change working conditions, assist refugees, and improve agriculture among other things. The Council has 54 members elected by the General Assembly for 3-year terms. It meets semi-annually and decisions are by majority vote.

The Trusteeship Council. The Trusteeship council is responsible for the oversight of territories that are under UN protection and not yet independent nations. Most of these were former colonies such as Cameroon and New Guinea. There were eleven of these trusteeships at the end of World War II. Most are now independent nations.

Answer true or false.

1.7 _____ The UN has its own army to enforce its decisions.

1.8 _____ The Soviets could veto any UN resolution.

1.9 _____ The General Assembly has oversight of territories under UN protection.

1.10 _____ The Secretary-General is a figurehead.

1.11 _____ The Security Council is responsible for keeping peace in the world.

Answer the question.

1.12 What are the strengths and weaknesses of the United Nations?

_____

_____

_____

_____

_____

Marshall Plan. Much of Europe was so devastated by World War II that people were willing to vote the communists into power if they promised jobs and food. Faced with this threat, the United States began a massive program of aid in 1948 aimed at helping countries recover from the war. It was called the Marshall Plan after Secretary of State, former General, George Marshall who organized it. The countries of Eastern Europe were even invited to participate, but the Soviet Union would not allow that. Eventually, over 12 billion dollars provided the push Europe needed to return to prosperity and none of the free countries which participated became communist.

NATO. Forced to recognize the continuing threat the Soviet Union posed in Europe the United States decided to join in a peacetime military alliance for the first time in its history. The alliance was called **NATO**, the North Atlantic Treaty Organization. It was formed in 1949 by the nations of the United States, Canada, Iceland, Norway, Britain, the Netherlands, Denmark, Belgium, Luxembourg, Portugal, France, Italy, Greece, and Turkey. West Germany (created from the non-Soviet occupation zones) joined later. The pact basically warned the Soviets that any attack on one of these nations would be considered an attack on all of them. The allied nations contributed troops and supplies to maintain a combined army in Europe, ready to defend it. The Soviets responded by forming the **Warsaw Pact**, which claimed to be an alliance between the Soviet Union and its satellites, eventually including East Germany (created from the Soviet zone).

China. World War II had temporarily interrupted a civil war in China. Fighting between the communists, led by Mao Zedong, and the Nationalists, led by Chiang Kai-shek, resumed as soon as the departure of the Japanese occupation forces gave them elbow room. The communists re-entered the conflict with a great advantage. The Soviet Union had declared war on Japan two days before it surrendered. This was done at the request of the American government which had expected to need help defeating the Japanese Empire. The success of the atomic bomb allowed the Soviets to capture north China without much effort. The Soviets gave Mao Zedong's forces this industrial rich northern area. The Soviet Union also gave them the weapons and supplies captured from the Japanese. Moreover, the Nationalists suffered from the corruption and ineptitude so common in traditional Chinese government. The United States refused to give the Nationalists much assistance believing there was little they could do to affect the outcome.

The communists, with widespread popular support from the long oppressed peasants, quickly gained the upper hand. Late in 1949, the Nationalists and their supporters fled to the island of Formosa (Taiwan) and established themselves there. On the mainland, Mao announced the formation of the People's Republic of China.

This was a frightening development for the United States which feared a Chinese-Soviet Communist alliance. Until 1978 the United States did not recognize Mao's government and considered the leaders of Taiwan to be the legitimate government of China. In fact, the Soviets and the Chinese did cooperate for a time, but dictators seldom cooperate well. The two countries eventually were publicly disagreeing with each other and even fought skirmishes along their mutual border.

Complete the following.

1.13   The U.S. feared that communist China would ally itself with _____ .

1.14   The first defensive alliance the United States ever entered into was _____ .

1.15   The United States gave substantial aid to Europe after World War II under the _____

_____ .

1.16   The two parties in China's civil war were _____ and

_____ .

1.17   _____ was the victorious Chinese leader in 1949.

Answer the statement.

1.18   Why did China fall to the communists?

_____

_____

_____

_____

THE COURSE OF THE COLD WAR

Berlin Blockade. The Cold War was defined by a series of crises and local wars much like a regular war is defined by battles. The first "battle" of the Cold War came over Berlin. Berlin, like Germany as a whole, had been divided into four separate zones each occupied by a different Allied nation (United States, Britain, France, and the Soviet Union). This division, which was intended to be very temporary, was still officially in place when the Cold War ended. The difficulty was that Berlin was located deep inside the Soviet occupation zone. Therefore, the western nations had to send supplies to their parts of the city through the Soviet zone. In 1948, The Soviets refused to let the Allies cross their zone. They hoped to force the West to abandon Berlin to the communists. The United States refused, and instead organized a huge airlift to supply the city. At its height "Operation Vittles" was landing one plane in Berlin every three minutes around the clock. The Soviets finally admitted the West was not going to give up Berlin and ended the blockade after almost a year.

Nuclear Arms Race. The year 1949 was a dark one for the United States. Not only did China fall to the communists that year, but the Soviet Union also exploded its first atomic bomb. American experts had not expected that development for several more years. The Soviet Union presumably used spies to steal the information on several key parts of the bomb from the United States. This development set up one of the defining features of the Cold War, the nuclear arms race. Both of the superpowers were afraid of the other achieving nuclear superiority. The United States was particularly concerned because communism placed no value on human life. Communists considered all methods acceptable to advance their goals. Therefore, both superpowers committed huge resources to developing newer, stronger bombs and faster ways to deliver them. The United States exploded its first **thermonuclear** bomb in 1952. The Soviet Union did the same in 1953. Later in the 1950's, both sides developed **intercontinental ballistic missiles** (ICBMs) and equipped submarines with nuclear weapons.

Both sides eventually built enough weapons to destroy each other several times over. The sheer number and power of these weapons justifiably frightened planners in both nations. There was good reason to fear that a war between the superpowers might escalate to include nuclear weapons. If that happened, the two sides might destroy not only each other, but the rest of the world too. This was one of the primary reasons that the Cold War stayed cold.

Korean War. The Soviet Union had occupied the nation of Korea north of the 38th parallel of north latitude in the closing days of World War II. In keeping with his actions in Eastern Europe, Stalin refused to allow Korea to be reunited under a free government. Instead he set up a communist government in North Korea, while the United States allowed free elections in South Korea. Both north and south claimed to be the lawful government for the entire nation. The United States ended its occupation of the south in 1949 and withdrew its troops.

On June 25, 1950, North Korea invaded the South. The United Nations immediately condemned the invasion and asked its members to aid South Korea. The Soviet Union would have vetoed this action, but it was boycotting to protest the fact that Communist China had not been given the Chinese seat on the UN Security Council. Without ever formally declaring war, the United States provided most of the men and weapons for the conflict that followed.

The North quickly drove the unprepared South Korean troops down the Korean Peninsula. American reinforcements did not arrive quickly enough to prevent the fall of the capital, Seoul. In fact, the Allies (U.S., South Korea, and other UN members) were driven back until they held only a small area around the city of Pusan in the country's southeast corner. There they held their ground at what was known as the Pusan Perimeter.

General Douglas MacArthur was given command of the Allies. He decided not to fight his way back up the peninsula through the enemy lines. Instead, in a brilliant military maneuver, he sent troops to land halfway up the peninsula at Inchon, near Seoul. These forces cut off the army attacking the Pusan Perimeter and liberated the capital. Then, MacArthur began to drive up into North Korea. Allied forces had almost conquered the entire country when China sent hundreds of thousands of "volunteers" to the aid of the North Koreans. It was the Allies who were then driven back. They lost and then later retook Seoul in the fighting that followed. The conflict eventually reached a stalemate very near the 38th parallel which had been the original border.

MacArthur wanted to attack China and he became very public about his opinion. President Truman, however, was worried about starting World War III and insisted on keeping the war in Korea. This approach is known as a "limited war." When MacArthur continued to publicly work against the policies of his commander-in-chief, Truman fired him. MacArthur had tremendous support at home. Truman's decision made him very unpopular. Many people still believe that MacArthur was correct in his opinions, but it was not his decision to make.

A cease-fire was proposed in June of 1951. Truce talks began in July. Both sides quickly agreed on a new dividing line between North and South Korea. However, the talks stalled over the issue of **repatriation** of prisoners of war. Many of the Chinese and North Korean prisoners did not want to be forced to return to their communist homelands. The communists insisted that all prisoners had to be repatriated even if it was against their will. The Allies refused. The talks stalled until March of 1953. The impasse was broken when Joseph Stalin died and the new Soviet leaders decided to support the truce.

An armistice was signed in July of 1953 ending the fighting, but not officially ending the war. A two and a half mile wide **Demilitarized Zone** was set up along the border of the two nations. Prisoners who did not wish to return home could be visited by delegates from their nation, but would not be forced to return. Over 14,000 Chinese and over 7,000 North Koreans did not go home. A much smaller number of South Koreans and even a few Americans also refused. The war ended much as it had begun with the communists holding most of Korea north of the 38th parallel. They had not gained any new ground. In accordance with U.S. policy, communism had been "contained."

Answer these following.

1.19 Why was Douglas MacArthur fired as commander of the armed forces in Korea?

_____

_____

_____

1.20 What two things happened in 1949 that were victories for communism?

a. _____

b. _____

1.21 Why was there good reason to fear a war between the United States and the Soviet Union?

_____

_____

_____

1.22 How did the United States respond to the Berlin Blockade?

_____

_____

_____

1.23 What issue stalled the peace talks to end the Korean War?

_____

_____

_____

1.24 What did the Korean War accomplish?

_____

_____

_____

1.25 What was MacArthur's strategy to break out of the Pusan Perimeter and how did it work?

_____

_____

_____

> **Write** *true* **or** *false*.

1.26   _____   The Allies were initially driven back in Korea, but held at the Pusan Perimeter.

1.27   _____   The nuclear arms race was one of the defining features of the Cold War.

1.28   _____   The U.S. Congress declared war on North Korea shortly after the invasion of the South began.

1.29   _____   Korea was a limited war.

Changes after Stalin's death. After Stalin died in 1953, Nikita Khrushchev gradually assumed the dominant role in the Soviet Union. This brought about a change in Soviet tactics. The communists still sought to take over the world, but from this point on the Soviets began to be more cautious. They began to negotiate with the United States over issues of trade and armaments. The new leadership definitely did not want to start a nuclear war. But, tension between the two powers continued and crises still occurred. Relations between the superpowers went up and down like a roller coaster for the rest of the Cold War. Discussions and agreements would bring "thaws" and the next crisis would return to the Cold War "chill." Moreover, the Soviets made it very clear that they intended to retain control of Eastern Europe.

Invasion of Hungary. The communist dictator of Hungary, Matthias Rákosi, did a great deal of damage to the nation's economy in the years after World War II. Due to discontent, he allowed a more liberal man, Imre Nagy to become premier in 1953. However, Rákosi did not like the reforms Nagy instituted and removed him from office in 1955. The reversal caused more discontent which roared into open revolt in October of 1956. Nagy was reappointed and established a reform, anti-communist government. Soviet troops invaded within days. They used tanks against the protesters. Nagy was executed, a hard line communist government was installed, and about 200,000 people fled the country. The Soviet Union had no intention of losing its satellites. The United States did what it could to help the refugees, including allowing 30,000 to immigrate to this country.

Suez Crisis. President Gamal Abdel Nasser of Egypt sought funds from the west to build a huge dam on the upper Nile River during the mid 1950's. The United States offered to fund the project until Nasser began to accept aid from the Soviet Union. Then, the offer was withdrawn. Furious, Nasser took over the Suez Canal, which was owned by British and French investors, intending to use its revenue to finance the dam. This action threatened the supply of oil to the United States and Europe.

Israel, France, and Britain staged a joint attack on Egypt in October of 1956 while the Soviet army was busy with Hungary. The United States was not informed of the attack until it began. The Soviet Union threatened to send troops to help Egypt. With American backing, the United Nations was able to negotiate a cease fire and sent in its first peace keeping troops to maintain order. The Soviets eventually provided the money to build the Aswan High Dam.

The Soviet support of Egypt set a pattern for the Cold War. The Soviets became the usual source of weapons and aid for the more aggressive Arab nations. This was especially true of the violent Arab terrorist groups that were often trained as well as supplied by the communists. At the same time, the United States supported Israel and some of the more moderate Arab nations in the Middle East.

Incidents and problems. The Soviet Union set off a panic in the United States when it launched the first artificial satellite into Earth's orbit, Sputnik I, in 1957 and successfully tested an ICBM the same year. America immediately stepped up its own rocket and space programs. An American satellite was successfully launched in January of 1958 re-establishing the balance of technology.

A thaw occurred in 1959 when the super power leaders met several times to engage in friendly discussions. This thaw was ruined by the U-2 Incident in May of 1960. An American U-2 spy plane was shot down that month over the Soviet Union. The pilot was captured and confessed to being on a photographic spy mission. President Dwight Eisenhower admitted that the United States was regularly flying spy missions over Soviet territory and refused to apologize. Further discussions planned between the two powers were canceled as a result.

Cuba. The island nation of Cuba is about 90 miles south of Florida. In 1959, a revolutionary group led by Fidel Castro overthrew the island's dictator and formed a new government. At first the United States supported the change. But, beginning in 1960 Castro began to seize American businesses and property in Cuba. The United States responded by cutting off trade and diplomatic relations with the

the island. Castro answered by establishing trade relations with the Soviet Union and setting up a communist government. The United States was deeply concerned about having a communist neighbor.

Bay of Pigs. Many Cubans who opposed Castro fled to the United States as his policies became clear. These exiles organized an invasion of their homeland to overthrow the Castro dictatorship. The exiles were trained in Central America by the CIA (Central Intelligence Agency of the United States) and promised American fighter cover for the invasion. President Kennedy approved of the invasion. However, he refused to send military planes to protect the exiles as they landed at the Bay of Pigs in April of 1961. Without proper support, the exiles were squashed by Castro's forces. The entire fiasco damaged American prestige, especially in Latin America.

Cuban Missile Crisis. Castro was convinced by 1962 that the United States would eventually invade Cuba. He, therefore, arranged with the Soviets to install nuclear missiles in Cuba aimed at the United States. These would be in easy range of the major American cities of the east coast. Besides protecting Cuba, the weapons could be used to blackmail the United States in other areas of the world. By God's provision, the United States learned of the missile bases before they were completed. (They were picked up on reconnaissance photos).

President John F. Kennedy ordered a blockade of Cuba to prevent the missiles from being delivered. He then demanded the removal of the bases already in place. For several very tense days no one knew if the Soviets would honor the blockade or start a war over it. Finally, the Soviet ships carrying the missiles turned back and Khrushchev agreed to remove the bases, over Castro's protests. In exchange, the United States agreed not to invade Cuba.

Berlin Wall. Berlin, Germany was still an occupied city divided into four zones in 1961. The World War II allies had not been able to reach an agreement on the reunification of the city and the country. The Soviet held part of the city and nation had been made into a nominally independent communist dictatorship. It was called the German Democratic Republic or East Germany. The western held sectors had formed a republic named the Federal Republic of Germany or West Germany. West Germany, unlike its eastern counterpart, had regained its prosperity with the aid of the Marshall Plan. Political and economic conditions in East Germany were so bad that almost 3 million citizens fled to the West. Most of the people fled through Berlin because the communists had closed the rest of the border between the two nations. Facing a massive loss of workers, especially educated people, the communists moved to stop the flood of refugees in August of 1961. In that month they literally built a wall around the city of West Berlin to keep East Germans from reaching freedom there. Germans in the west called it *Schandmauer* (wall of shame). To most of the world, it was the Berlin Wall, the most infamous symbol of the Cold War.

Berlin Wall before 1989

♣ **Answer these questions.**

1.30   What ruined the American–Soviet thaw of 1959?

_____

_____

_____

1.31   What nations attacked Egypt in 1956 to recover the Suez Canal?

a. _____   c. _____

b. _____

9

1.32   Why was the Berlin Wall put up?

_____

_____

_____

1.33   What happened at the Bay of Pigs in 1961?

_____

_____

_____

1.34   Why did the U.S. blockade Cuba in 1962?

_____

_____

_____

1.35   What triggered the Soviet invasion of Hungary in 1956?

_____

_____

_____

Match the following.

1.36   _____ Sputnik   a. Made Cuba communist

1.37   _____ Nasser   b. Seized the Suez Canal

1.38   _____ Krushchev   c. A more cautious Soviet leader

1.39   _____ Kennedy   d. World's first man-made satellite

1.40   _____ Castro   e. Ordered the blockade of Cuba

Vietnam War. The southeast Asian nations of Vietnam, Cambodia, and Laos were part of French Indochina before World War II. After the war the French tried to reconquer their former colony. They were opposed by a communist group, the Vietminh, led by a Vietnamese man named Ho Chi Minh. The United States aided the French effort as part of their world wide fight against communism. In 1954, the French were defeated and a peace treaty was signed in Geneva, Switzerland. The treaty arranged for the country to be divided temporarily at the 17th parallel until elections could be held.

Ho Chi Minh set up a communist government in the northern sector. The southern leader, Ngo Dinh Diem, refused to allow elections because of the communist track record of ignoring or subverting them and because he preferred to remain in power. The United States agreed with Diem and began sending him aid. Diem was a corrupt and autocratic ruler who quickly alienated the peasant population of his nation. Moreover, the communists had many supporters in South Vietnam who had fought for independence against the French. In 1957, the South Vietnamese communists, the Viet Cong, rebelled against Diem with the support of North Vietnam. The North, in turn, received aid from the Soviet Union and China. The United States began sending more aid and military advisors to Diem's government.

Diem's misgovernment continued to worsen. In the early 1960's, he began to face protests from the majority Buddhists in his country (Diem was Roman Catholic) accusing him of curtailing their religion. The situation reached crisis proportions when the government began raids on the Buddhist temples. When Diem refused to listen to reason, President Kennedy began supporting a group of opposition South Vietnamese generals. They staged a military coup in 1963. Diem was killed. The new government proved to be corrupt, unstable, and unable to win the support of the people who viewed it as an American creation.

American soldiers in Vietnam

Supporting this unpopular and unstable government, the United States began to take a larger and larger role in the war. In 1964 two American destroyers were reportedly fired upon by the North Vietnamese in the Gulf of Tonkin. (They were secretly supporting South Vietnamese raids on the North). President Lyndon Johnson used this incident to request Congressional support for an even wider American role in the fighting. On August 7, 1964 the congress passed the Gulf of Tonkin Resolution which gave the president extensive authority to increase U.S. involvement. In March of 1965 the first American ground troops were sent in to fight.

The American troops were far better equipped and supplied than the communist guerrillas they fought. However, they could not defeat an enemy who fought, faded away, and mixed in with the general population. The United States did extensive bombing in North Vietnam in an unsuccessful attempt to cut off supplies to the Viet Cong. However, in keeping with the policy of limited warfare, no attempt was made to conquer North Vietnam. There will always be a question about this policy. Such an invasion might have truly ended the war or it might have started World War III when the Soviets and Chinese came to North Vietnam's aid.

The war was, therefore, effectively fought to a draw with neither side able to gain a definite advantage. The South Vietnamese people were faced with the massive destruction of their land and population as the war dragged on. The continuing instability and unpopularity of the South Vietnamese government forced the United States to run the war itself. The cost and casualties began to grow alarmingly. By the end of the 1960's, the United States had over a half a million men fighting in Vietnam. (About 47,000 men died during the war.) In America, an increasingly liberal and political youth movement found a cause in opposing the war. Mass protests, anti-war slogans, and opposition to the **draft** made the war a difficult political issue as well as a military one.

In January of 1968, the Viet Cong launched a massive attack which coincided with the beginning of Tet, the Vietnamese New Year celebration. The Tet Offensive was thrown back by the United States and the South Vietnamese. The Viet Cong suffered massive casualties. However, the sheer size of the attack was a shock to the United States. No one had believed the Viet Cong were capable of mounting such a large, well coordinated military offensive. Faced with such a capable and resolute enemy as well as mounting opposition at home, President Johnson authorized peace negotiations.

These negotiations failed, but the United States began to reduce its commitment to the war. President Richard Nixon began a policy of Vietnamization in 1969. This policy called for the training of South Vietnamese troops to gradually take over the war for themselves. The withdrawal of American troops was begun in the same year. However, fighting continued and even intensified as supply areas in neutral Cambodia were attacked in 1970. In 1972, the North Vietnamese launched a major invasion of the South. U.S. bombing and mining of Northern harbors helped to stop the invasion, but the costs were high on both sides.

Peace talks were re-opened in Paris after the failed invasion. An agreement was signed in January of 1973. It allowed for return of prisoners, withdrawal of American troops, and internationally monitored elections to decide the fate of the entire nation. The elections were never held. Fighting began again after the last American troops left. Congress continued to reduce the aid sent to the South Vietnamese government. The North Vietnamese increased their attacks in the light of U.S. pacificism. As communist troops swept into South Vietnam, Congress refused to send aid to its former ally. American citizens and many desperate South Vietnamese fled the country. The capital, Saigon, fell in April of 1975 and was renamed Ho Chi Minh City.

The loss of Vietnam and the controversy that surrounded it marked America. America has since been a more cynical nation, less willing to trust both its leaders and itself. The policy of containment officially continued, but Americans were less sure of their role in the Cold War.

Vietnam War Veterans Memorial Wall Washington, D.C.

✳ **Choose the correct letter.**

1.41	_____ Viet Cong	a. North Vietnamese communists
1.42	_____ Ho Chi Minh	b. Vietnamese communist leader
1.43	_____ Vietminh	c. Corrupt South Vietnamese leader
1.44	_____ Nixon	d. Asked Congress to support wider American involvement
1.45	_____ Johnson	e. South Vietnamese communists
1.46	_____ Ngo Dinh Diem	f. Began policy of Vietnamization

✿ Complete the statement.

1.47   Vietnam, like Korea, was a _____ war.

1.48   The _____ was passed by Congress in 1964 and allowed the president to expand American involvement in Vietnam.

1.49   Saigon was renamed _____ after the fall of South Vietnam.

1.50   _____ refused to send aid to South Vietnam as it was invaded in 1975.

1.51   The _____ was a well coordinated, large scale Viet Cong attack that began during the Vietnamese New Year celebration.

Invasion of Czechoslovakia. The economy of Czechoslovakia had done poorly under communism. By the 1960's many voices, even within the government, were calling for reform. In 1968 a reform minded man by the name of Alexander Dubček became the communist party leader. He instituted a series of reforms that became known as the Prague Spring. The other communist leaders in Europe became nervous as Czechoslovakia increased personal freedoms and decreased controls. In August of 1968, troops from the Soviet Union and four Warsaw Pact nations invaded. The Soviet troops remained and the reforms were reversed. The government was a faithful Soviet ally for the remainder of the Cold War.

Détente. China and the Soviet Union came into conflict with each other increasingly as the 1950's ended. Mao Zedong, China's dictator, was a true believer in communism. He tried repeatedly to make China a classless, revolutionary society and did great damage in the process. He thought the Soviet Union's willingness to negotiate with the West was a betrayal of communism and a threat to the security of China. In 1960 the Soviet Union stopped sending China technical assistance. After the United States and the Soviet Union signed a nuclear test ban treaty in 1963, China broke off relations with the Soviet Union. The two nations fought each other in a series of border clashes in 1969.

The United States realized that it could use the communist split to play the two communist powers off against each other. In 1972 President Richard Nixon made a historic trip to Communist China. Although it accomplished little in terms of results, the meeting began to open the door to that previously closed nation. Unfortunately, this also led to the recognition of the People's Republic of China as the real government of the nation in 1979. This was unfortunate because in doing so the United States ceased to recognize the government of Taiwan which had been an American ally for so long.

Relations between the United States and the Soviet Union continued to improve during this period of time. Nixon also visited Moscow to discuss cuts in the awesome nuclear arms race between the two nations. Several agreements were reached under a series of Strategic Arms Limitation Talks (SALT). A second group of agreements, SALT II, was signed in 1979, but never ratified because of the Soviet invasion of Afghanistan in that year. This period of thaw was called *détente*. It comes from the French word for loosening and refers to an easing of tensions between nations.

Invasion of Afghanistan. Afghanistan is a small Islamic nation located just south of Turkmenistan, Uzekistan, and Tajikistan. In 1979 those nations were part of the Soviet Union and Afghanistan was a tempting target on the southern border of the Soviet Union. A pro-Soviet faction had taken control of the Afghan government in 1978 in a bloody coup. In 1979, the Soviet Union sent in troops to support another coup that installed a more solidly communist regime. These troops spread out over the nation to insure the establishment of a successful communist government. They were met by determined resistance from Muslim rebels who effectively fought a guerrilla war much like the Viet Cong had in southeast Asia.

This aggression chilled relations with the United States instantly. It was proof that the fine words and careful advances of *détente* had not changed Soviet goals or methods. The United States halted sales of grain to the Soviet Union and refused to participate in the 1980 Olympics in Moscow. The United States also sent extensive aid to the Islamic guerrillas who successfully harassed the Soviet troops, killing perhaps 15,000 of them over a nine-year period. The Soviet Union never gained control of the rugged Afghan countryside. In 1988, the Soviet Union accepted a UN mediated agreement and withdrew its soldiers by February of 1989.

Solidarity. Poland, like most of the East European nations, was only communist because the Soviet Union would not allow otherwise. The indestructible Roman Catholic Church in Poland gave the people there a source of strength that was increased in 1978 when a Polish cardinal, Karol Wojiyla, became Pope John Paul II. Poland's economic condition in the late 1970's was poor. The nation suffered from high prices and a shortage of consumer goods that was **endemic** to communist regimes.

A huge, nationwide strike by workers demanding better pay, free trade unions, and political reforms took place in 1980 and spread rapidly. The communist government decided to meet most of the demands and in November recognized the first free (non-government) trade union in a communist nation, Solidarity. Solidarity was led by an electrician named Lech Walesa.

Walesa continued to demand economic and political reforms as the country's economy deteriorated in 1980-81. In December of 1981, under pressure from the Soviet Union to control his country, Wojciech Jaruzelski, head of the communist party, declared martial law and arrested the leaders of Solidarity. In October of the following year, he outlawed the organization entirely. The leaders were not killed, however. They were slowly released over the next few years as the government became more certain of its control.

Solidarity caught the imagination of the West. Many people thought that a communist nation would finally break free of its chains. The imposition of martial law was yet another indication of how committed the communists were to maintaining their autocratic system. Thus, *détente* had collapsed and many felt that the Cold War would never end. However, they did not know God's plans.

✚ **Answer these questions.**

1.52   What was Solidarity?

_____

_____

_____

1.53   What was the Prague Spring and how did it end?

_____

_____

_____

1.54   What were the positive and negative results of the American overtures toward China in the early 1970's?

_____

_____

_____

1.55   Why did the Soviets invade Afghanistan?

_____

_____

_____

1.56   How did the United States react to the Afghan invasion?

_____

_____

1.57   What is *Détente*?

_____

_____

1.58   How did the communists stop Solidarity?

_____

_____

_____

1.59   What was SALT and what did it accomplish?

_____

_____

THE END OF THE COLD WAR

Mikhail Gorbachev. Nikita Khrushchev had been removed from power and "retired" in 1964. He was replaced by Leonid Brezhnev who died in 1982. The next two Soviet leaders died very quickly, Yuri V. Andropov in 1984, and Konstantin U. Chernenko in 1985. In 1985 the youngest member of the ruling Politburo, Mikhail Gorbachev, was chosen to be the seventh leader of the Union of Soviet Socialist Republics. He was to be the last.

Gorbachev was young enough that he was not in the Party during the **purges** under Stalin. Stalin basically had killed off any capable person in the party who might eventually challenge his power. Thus, Gorbachev was not of the non-thinking, bureaucratic type which were the only survivors of Stalin's capricious anger.

Gorbachev recognized how far the Soviet Union was falling behind the United States in technology and infrastructure. He also realized the Soviet economy was in trouble. Communism did not reward good workers and the economy barely functioned. Moreover, the cost of maintaining the Soviet military machine (mired in Afghanistan at the time) and supporting pro-communist groups worldwide was staggering. He also seemed to genuinely favor reforming the bleak, restrictive Soviet society. In any case, Gorbachev began a series of startling reforms that changed the world.

Gorbachev allowed a policy of political reform called *glasnost* (openness). He began a series of economic reforms known as *perestroika* (restructuring). Gorbachev met several times with then president of the United States, Ronald Reagan, and signed an agreement to eliminate certain types of nuclear weapons in Europe. Gorbachev also allowed the people a choice of candidates in elections for a restructured Soviet government. All of the candidates came from the communist party, but they represented different factions and those favoring reform were elected in greater numbers. Gorbachev withdrew Soviet troops from Afghanistan, promised to reduce the military budget, and made it clear the Soviet Union would no longer use force to support communist governments in Eastern Europe.

The United States responded very cautiously to the Gorbachev storm. President Reagan was a staunch anti-communist who knew their reputation for deceit. He met with the new Soviet leader and welcomed the reforms. However, he continued to maintain American military readiness and was unwilling to assume the Cold War was over. The world press began to portray Gorbachev as a peacemaker and Reagan as the aggressor in the still running conflict. In fact, there was a large group of communists in the Soviet Union who were opposed to Gorbachev's reforms. The reforms would end if he fell from power and that was a very real possibility.

Revolution of 1989. The conservative communists in the Soviet Union received an unbelievable shock in 1989. Eastern Europe had endured the chains of communism since World War II. They would endure them no longer. Protests against communist rule broke out all over the Communist Block. The East European governments began to listen or fall.

Hungary began by exonerating the leaders of their 1956 revolt against the communists. Then, the government voted to increase personal freedom and allow the formation of other political parties, making Hungary a multi-party democracy, not a communist dictatorship.

Hungary also opened its border with Austria. Thousands of East Germans took advantage of this to go through Hungary and Austria to freedom in West Germany. East Germany faced again the crisis of a massive loss of population. In November of 1989, East Germany accepted the inevitable and opened its border with the West. In Berlin, people began to climb over the "Wall of Shame." Guards no longer shot them for doing it. Armed with sledgehammers, picks, hammers, and anything else they could find, the people of Berlin began to tear down the Wall. The entire world watched in awe to see it fall. With a rapidity that was nothing short of astonishing, Germany was reunited as one nation in October of 1990.

Mikhail Gorbachev of the USSR

A transition government was formed in Czechoslovakia after massive street protests. The government was lead by a dissident playwright, Václav Havel. It smoothly ran the government until free elections in 1990 put non-communists in power. In 1992, the nation split into two parts, the Czech Republic and Slovakia, which reflected the ethnic differences. The events were named "the Velvet Revolution" and "the Velvet Divorce."

The cruel, communist dictator of Romania was executed in 1989 after rebels from his own army rose against him. The dictator of Bulgaria was forced to resign and imprisoned for corruption. Both countries held free elections in 1990.

The governments of Yugoslavia and Albania followed with free elections in 1990 and 1991. Albanians fled from their poverty-strickened country by the thousands in the early 1990's to seek better economic conditions elsewhere. Yugoslavia, which was home to several ethnic groups which hated each other, split into five nations in 1991. These new countries rapidly became entangled in civil wars between the various groups who competed for control of the land. The Serbs of Bosnia-Herzegovina were especially aggressive and inhumane in their lust for territory. By the mid-1990's the wars had killed thousands and driven thousands of others from their homes.

The destruction of the Berlin Wall was the key point for the end of communism in Eastern Europe. It was the most significant symbol of the division of Europe between Free and Communist. The United States welcomed the events of 1989 and was delighted when the Soviet Union did not interfere. However, the U.S.S.R. was still officially communist and very powerful. Many knowledgeable people were concerned that the matter was not yet settled.

● ●

★ **Complete the statement.**

1.60   Gorbachev's two key reforms were _____ and
_____ .

1.61   _____ led the transition government in Czechoslovakia.

1.62   The dictator of _____ was executed after a rebellion by the army.

1.63   _____ split into five nations after the fall of communism.

1.64   The event that marks the end of communism in Eastern Europe was the destruction of
_____ .

1.65   East Germany opened its borders with the west because so many of its people were
_____ .

✦ **Answer** *true* **or** *false*.

1.66   _____ Hungary continues to look at the leaders of their 1956 revolt as criminals.

1.67   _____ Gorbachev was the youngest member of the Politburo when he was chosen to lead the Soviet Union.

1.68   _____ The United States was cautious about believing Gorbachev's reforms were permanent.

1.69   _____ Albania was an unusually prosperous communist nation that suffered no substantial population loss when its borders were opened.

1.70   _____ The two Germanys began negotiations to reunite, but had not come to terms by the mid-1990's.

Fall of the Soviet Union. The Soviet Union consisted of fifteen "republics" rather like provinces or states. The government of the republic of Russia quickly became very reform-minded after Gorbachev's perestroika. It was led by Boris Yeltsin. Yeltsin had the distinction of being thrown out of the Soviet Politburo in 1987 for advocating radical economic reform. He won his presidency in a contested election in 1991. He rapidly became a popular and powerful figure, especially since Gorbachev had not been freely elected to any post.

In August of 1991, the Republics were to sign a new Union treaty which would give them greater **autonomy**. The conservatives, however, had had enough. Led by Gorbachev's Vice-President the anti-reform communists took control of the government in Moscow. They confined Gorbachev at his country home and declared a state of emergency. Boris Yeltsin called on the people to oppose the coup. Thousands demonstrated in support of him and many of the army units refused to accept orders from the "emergency" government. The coup collapsed in three days. Gorbachev was restored, but Yeltsin was now the real power in the Soviet Union.

Immediately after the coup, all activities of the communist party were suspended in the Soviet Union. Yeltsin ordered his people to take control of all government functions within the Russian Republic. In November, Yeltsin banned the communist party in Russia and seized its assets. By the end of the year, the republics had decided that they did not want a new central government over them. Instead, they agreed to form a loose confederation. On December 25, 1991 Mikhail Gorbachev resigned as the last President of the Union of Soviet Socialist Republics. The following day the Soviet Union was formally dissolved and the Commonwealth of Independent States which comprised eleven of the fifteen former republics took its place.

After the fall. Reforms in the new Commonwealth countries have been hampered by rising crime rates, widespread unemployment, and a simple lack of knowledge on how to run private businesses. There have been several conflicts between ethnic groups in the new countries. A power struggle between Yeltsin and the Russian parliament (still dominated by former communists) resulted in the army being called in to seize the Parliament building in 1993. However, the most striking change in the former Soviet Union has been spiritual. There is a deep, insatiable hunger for the Word of God in Russia. Many people have become Christians. However, many cults are exploiting this hunger to their own advantage. Moreover, The Russian Orthodox Church (which survived the communist era by cooperating with the government) seeks to exclude all who are not of its faith. The challenges are many for these people who have known only slavery and spiritual darkness for their entire lives.

Conclusion. The United States won the Cold War. It was a victory that went to the survivor. It left behind a huge debt, a massive caché of nuclear weapons, and a freer world. The long struggle exhausted both of the superpowers. However, the vital, free American economy was able to survive the pressure. The post-Cold War world is a very complicated place. It is not clear what new alliances will rise out of its ashes. This is where our record of history stops and you begin to observe history as it is made.

Complete the following.

1.71 _____ was the elected president of Russia who lead the resistance to the communist coup in 1991.

1.72 The communist coup attempt collapsed in _____ days.

1.73 What are the problems that face the counties of the former Soviet Union?

_____

_____

_____

1.74 _____ was thrown out of the Politburo in 1987 for advocating rapid reforms.

1.75   Why did the coup attempt by the communists fail in 1991?

_____

_____

_____

1.76   Eleven of the original fifteen republics of the Soviet Union formed the
         _____ in 1991.

◆◆   **Complete this activity.**

       You have studied the reality of communism in this LIFEPAC. Research the theory of communism
       as it was written by Marx. Then answer these two questions (one page each).

1.77   Why were people attracted by communism?
1.78   What are the flaws you can find in communist *theory*?

Teacher check _____
                      Initial   Date

☀   Review the material in this section in preparation for the Self Test. The Self Test will check your
      mastery of this particular section. The items missed on this Self Test will indicate specific areas
      where restudy is needed for mastery.

SELF TEST 1

Choose the correct letter to identify the person. (2 points each answer)

1.01	_____	Joseph Stalin	a.	Last president of the U.S.S.R.
1.02	_____	Mao Zedong	b.	Leader of Solidarity
1.03	_____	Fidel Castro	c.	Egyptian president
1.04	_____	Ho Chi Minh	d.	Soviet leader, began the Cold War
1.05	_____	Lech Walesa	e.	American president during Cuban Missile
1.06	_____	Mikhail Gorbachev		Crisis
1.07	_____	Douglas MacArthur	f.	Cuban communist leader
1.08	_____	Gamal Abdel Nasser	g.	Chinese communist leader
1.09	_____	John F. Kennedy	h.	Korean War military commander
1.010	_____	Harry Truman	i.	Vietnamese communist leader
			j.	American president, formulated containment policy

Complete the sentence using the answers below. (2 points each answer)

Pusan Perimeter	Bay of Pigs	Sputnik
Détente	General Assembly	Warsaw Pact
SALT	Security Council	Solidarity
Gulf of Tonkin Resolution		

1.011   U.S. trained Cuban exiles tried to invade Cuba at the _____.

1.012   The first satellite ever launched into earth's orbit was the Soviet _____.

1.013   All countries in the United Nations are represented in the _____
_____.

1.014   The Cold War "thaw" of the 1970's was called _____.

1.015   The military alliance between the Soviet Union and its satellites was called
_____.

1.016   The UN _____ is responsible for world peace and has
five permanent members who have a veto over decisions.

1.017   The _____ gave the president extensive authority to
increase American involvement in the Vietnam War.

1.018   The first free trade union in a communist country was _____.

1.019   The initial invasion by the North Korean's in 1950 drove the Allied troops back to
_____.

1.020   _____ was a series of agreements between the superpowers to reduce
the number of nuclear weapons each held.

Complete the statement. (3 points each answer)

1.021   The most infamous symbol of the Cold War was the _____ which divided
the German capital.

1.022   The United States gave billions of dollars to rebuild post-World War II Europe under the
_____ to prevent communism from growing there.

1.023   The United States blockaded Cuba to prevent nuclear weapons from being installed there
during the _____.

1.024   The Soviets cut off access to Berlin by land during the _____;
so the city was supplied by air for almost a year.

1.025   The Western democracies formed a mutual defense alliance called
_____ after World War II to face the growing Soviet threat.

Complete this activity. (5 points)

1.026   Describe the American policy of containment.

_____

_____

_____

_____

Choose the correct country from the list below. (3 points each answer)

China   Poland   Czechoslovakia
Afghanistan   Soviet Union

1.027 _____ Communists drove out the Nationalists who took refuge on the island of Taiwan.

1.028 _____ Prague Spring of 1968 was crushed by the Warsaw Pact.

1.029 _____ A U-2 spy plane from the United States was shot down in 1960.

1.030 _____ Communists were never able to take full control of the country due to American backed Moslem rebels.

1.031 _____ The Catholic Church gave strength to the founders of Solidarity.

Choose one of the following topics and discuss it in a detailed paragraph. (25 points)

1.032 Fall of Communism in Eastern Europe
       The Causes and Course of the Korean War
       The Causes and Conclusion of the Vietnam War

_____

_____

_____

_____

_____

_____

_____

_____

_____

_____

_____

_____

_____

_____

_____

_____

_____

80 / 100

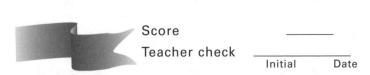

Score _____

Teacher check _____
            Initial   Date

II. THE WORLD TODAY

This section will present a continent by continent sketch of our world as of 1995. Obviously this is not intended to give you a tremendous amount of detail about each country's history since World War II. Instead, this overview will give you a place to start when you review subjects that are relevant in our world today. You will, for example, know something of the origins of the conflicts in the Middle East and Africa. A survey like this is a starting place for further investigation of topics that are important to you and your own interests.

SECTION OBJECTIVES

Read these objectives to learn what you should be able to do when you have completed this section.

6. Describe the basic geography of the six inhabited continents.

7. Name the major mountains, rivers, lakes, and deserts of the six inhabited continents.

8. Recognize the names and locations of the countries of the world.

9. Have a basic understanding of the current status of the nations of the world.

VOCABULARY

Study these words and phrases to enhance your learning success in this section. If you do not know the definition, look it up in a dictionary or encyclopedia.

deficit	federal republic	non-aligned
Third World	Latin America	*junta*
subsidies	nationalize	Gulf Stream
socialist	capitalism	apartheid
head of state	parliamentary democracy	

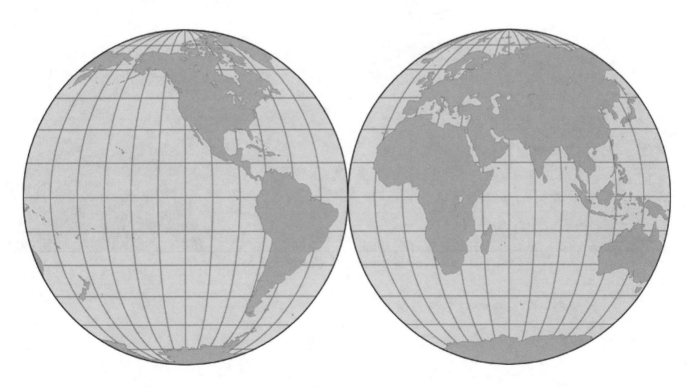

North American Continent

NORTH AMERICA

THE LAND

The continent of North America is a roughly triangular shaped land mass that stretches from the Arctic Circle to within a few degrees latitude of the Equator. It is bounded by the Pacific, Arctic, and Atlantic Oceans. It is the third largest continent covering about 9,363,000 square miles (24,249,000 square kilometers). It includes Greenland, the United States, Canada, Mexico, Central America, and the Caribbean Islands.

North America is connected to South America by the Isthmus of Panama. The two continents are technically separated by the man-made Panama Canal. The Isthmus itself takes a very sharp turn to the north before it connects with South America. This creates a geographic oddity. At one point in Panama you can start from the Pacific Ocean, walk due <u>west</u> on a straight line, and run into the Atlantic Ocean.

A long string of mountains run along the western side of the continent. They are called the Rocky Mountains north of Mexico and the Sierra Madre mountains in the south. The continent's tallest peak is Mount McKinley in Alaska (20,320 feet). The interior of the continent is a vast, fertile plain excellent for agriculture. This plain is watered by several rivers. The most extensive is the Mississippi River and its tributaries, which include the Missouri, Ohio, Red, Arkansas, and Platte Rivers. A series of connected lakes, known as the Great Lakes, lie at about 45 degrees north latitude on the eastern side of the central plains. One of these, Lake Superior, is the largest fresh water lake in the world. The lakes, which include lakes Michigan, Huron, Erie, and Ontario, feed the St. Lawrence River which empties into the Atlantic Ocean. A series of locks and channels allow ocean vessels to carry cargo down the river to the industrial cities that border the lakes. There is a second string of mountains called the Appalachians along the central east coast.

The climate of North America includes all known types. The interior of Greenland is covered by a permanent ice cap. Central America includes tropical rain forests. In between the two are arctic, desert, highland, subtropical, and other climates. Spanish, French, English, and Danish are spoken. The principle religions are various forms of Christianity. Thus, North America is a continent of much variety.

⇒ Complete the following.

2.1   North and South America are connected by the _____
     _____ .

2.2   The tallest mountain in North America is _____ .

2.3   The names of the Great Lakes are:

     a. _____   d. _____

     b. _____   e. _____

     c. _____

2.4   Central America (is/is not) _____ part of North America.

2.5   The most extensive river system of the central plains is the _____
     River and its tributaries.

2.6   The mountain ridge along North America's west coast is called the
     a. _____ north of Mexico and the b. _____
     from Mexico to the south.

THE NATIONS

Greenland. Greenland is part of the territory of Denmark. It has had home rule since 1979. Technically, Greenlandic names should be used for the land and cities; the nation's name is Kalaallit Nunaat.

Canada. Canada is a **parliamentary democracy** and, due to the fact it has maintained its ties with England, Queen Elizabeth II is the official **head of state**. Canada was a faithful ally of the United States during the Cold War and a charter member of NATO. The two nations share the longest unguarded border in the world.

They also have joined together with Mexico to sign the North American Free Trade Agreement (NAFTA). The agreement, which went into effect in 1994, will gradually reduce all tariffs between the three nations and create a continental free trade zone, if all of its goals are met. In the late 1980's to 1990's Canada has been convulsed by the repeated attempts of the French Canadians of Quebec to secede from the union. The vote in 1995 barely decided in favor of keeping Quebec as a part of Canada.

The United States. The United States remains the only superpower in the post–Cold War era. It is still considered the leader of the free, developed nations even though communism is no longer a threat. The United States was able, for example, to take the lead in freeing Kuwait from Iraqi invaders in the Persian Gulf War of 1990-91. However, it is trying to back off from its role as world policeman. The United States has a huge national debt and has run a budget **deficit** every year since 1969. That is partially due to the expenses of the Cold War. The United States' economy has been on a war footing for fifty years. It is a testament to the strength of the nation that it was not only able to do this, but did it while maintaining one of the highest standards of living in the world for its people. The United States as the only remaining superpower has to develop a delicate balance between its responsibilities abroad and those at home.

Mexico. Mexico is a **federal republic** which has been dominated by a single political party, the Institutional Revolutionary Party (known by its Spanish initials—PRI), since 1929. Mexico was a **non-aligned** nation during the Cold War. However, its proximity to the United States meant that any substantial communist activity there would have been considered a major threat by its powerful neighbor. Problems have developed with the United States over Mexican regulation of American companies, drug smuggling, and illegal immigration of Mexicans into the United States. However, close business ties, especially since the signing of NAFTA, have kept relations between the two neighbors relatively stable.

> **Complete the statement.**

2.7   The only remaining superpower in the world is _____ .

2.8   The dominant political party in Mexico is the _____ .

2.9   Elizabeth II of Britain is the head of state in _____ .

2.10   The proper name of Greenland is _____ .

2.11   The United States has run a budget _____ every year since 1969.

2.12   It is the goal of _____ to create a free trade zone between the nations of Mexico, the United States, and Canada.

CENTRAL AMERICA

The Central American region of the North American continent consists of the nations of Guatemala, El Salvador, Honduras, Belize, Nicaragua, Costa Rica, and Panama. This area was one of the many **Third World** battlegrounds during the Cold War. In 1948 all of these nations, except Belize (which was a British colony until 1981), joined with other **Latin American** nations and the United States to form the Organization of American States (OAS). This organization promotes cooperation among the member states. The Central American nations also formed an organization to promote free trade among themselves in the 1960's.

Latin American governments in the 20th century have often been run by a small group of very wealthy individuals while the majority of the population lived in stark poverty. Governments tended to be dictatorial and the military often intervened to take control. Due to the very uneven distribution of wealth, the people found the ideals of communism, which promised economic equality, appealing. The people were obviously not told about the harsh realities of a communist dictatorship. Moreover, the issue was further confused by the fact that genuine reformers were often labeled communist to discredit them. The United States was particularly nervous about communism developing so close to home. Thus, any anti-communist group tended to get American aid while any anti-American, pro-revolution group tended to get Soviet aid. Whoever was in power, the government was seldom fair or stable.

El Salvador and Nicaragua. The civil war in El Salvador from 1979-1992 was typical. Unrest in 1979 ended in a military take over of the government. The opponents of the military **junta** received aid from Cuba and the Soviet Union. So, the United States gave aid to the military government. A peace treaty was eventually signed in 1992 and free elections were held. The same type of thing occurred in Nicaragua. A pro-American dictatorial family ruled in that country from 1937-1979. They were overthrown by the Sandinista guerrillas who formed a new government. The Sandinistas aided the rebels in El Salvador and were receiving communist aid. So, the United States aided the rebel group in Nicaragua, the Contras. After the fall of communism in Eastern Europe, the Sandinistas held free elections and lost.

Other nations. Costa Rica has been a relatively stable country ruled primarily by elected presidents. It sought to be a non-aligned nation during the Cold War, but maintained good relations with the United States. Guatemala and Honduras have gone through numerous governments, elected and military, since World War II. Panama has been more stable, but the government has been dominated by the military. The last military strongman, Manuel Noriega, was overthrown by an American invasion in 1989. Noriega had invalidated the country's election results and was harassing American troops in the Panama Canal Zone. The Canal Zone and the Canal (built by the United States in the early 1900's) are being slowly transferred to Panamanian control under a 1977 treaty.

THE CARIBBEAN ISLANDS

The Caribbean Islands lie in an arc that runs from the northeast shore of Venezuela towards the Florida Peninsula. The major political entities are Cuba, Jamaica, Haiti, the Dominican Republic, Puerto Rico, and Trinidad & Tobago. Other islands include the Bahamas, the Virgin Islands, Barbados, Martinique, Grenada, and several more.

Cuba. Cuba was one of the most aggressive communist nations during the Cold War. It sent troops to aid "communist revolutions" all over the world. This suited the Soviet Union who could claim that Cuba was acting on its own.

Cuba was one of the few nations to still be communist as of the mid-1990's. Fidel Castro who led the revolution in 1959 was still in power and refused to allow his nation to follow the anti-communist tide. Like all nations that adhered to communist philosophy of state ownership of the means of production, Cuba's economy was very uncertain. Without incentives for better work, most people produced or grew only what was absolutely required. There were no surpluses that could be held for bad times. Cuba was also dependent upon **subsidies** from the Soviet Union which bought Cuban sugar at artificially high prices. Cuba's economy was severely damaged at the end by this and other benefits. Castro even allowed people to leave in 1994 to relieve some of the anti-government pressure. Such a flood of people left the island that the United States changed its long-standing policy and refused to allow them automatic entry into that country. As the Cuban economy declined, it was clear the government was more concerned about its power than its people.

The Dominican Republic, Haiti, and Jamaica. The Dominican Republic and Haiti share the island of Hispaniola. The Dominican Republic was ruled by a dictator from 1930-1961. The United States sent troops in to put down a revolt in 1966 that involved a few communists. Since that time, one man has dominated the government. Haiti is the world's oldest black republic and one of the poorest nations in the Western Hemisphere. The nation was ruled by the dictatorial Duvalier family for most of the Cold War. Since he was overthrown in 1986 there have been five governments. The president elected in 1990, Jean-Bertrand Aristide, was overthrown by the military and then returned to power under the threat of a U.S. invasion in 1994. Jamaica was a British colony that became a fully independent member of the British Commonwealth of Nations in 1962. It has been a relatively stable parliamentary democracy since that time.

Puerto Rico, Trinidad and Tobago, and other islands. Puerto Rico is a self-governing territory of the United States. It has repeatedly voted against either independence or statehood. Trinidad and Tobago are a pair of islands off Venezuela's coast that form one nation. It is a prosperous, oil producing parliamentary democracy. Grenada, another island, was invaded by the United States in 1983. The elected president had been overthrown by a pro-communist military coup. The island was defended primarily by Cuban advisors. The rest of the islands are either self governing territories or small independent republics.

Choose the correct letter.

2.13	_____ El Salvador	a.	Invaded by the U.S. in 1983
2.14	_____ Belize	b.	World's oldest black republic
2.15	_____ Haiti	c.	A British colony until 1981
2.16	_____ Trinidad & Tobago	d.	U.S. aided military *junta*
2.17	_____ Puerto Rico	e.	The Sandinistas vs. the Contras
2.18	_____ Grenada	f.	A parliamentary democracy since independence in
2.19	_____ Nicaragua		1962
2.20	_____ Jamaica	g.	A self-governing territory of the U.S.
		h.	Oil producing democracy

Answer the following.

2.21   Describe Cuba during the Cold War.

_____

_____

2.22   What did/did not change in Cuba as a result of the fall of the Soviet Union.

_____

_____

_____

2.23   What happened to the Haitian president elected in 1990?

_____

_____

_____

Answer the question.

2.24   Why it was sometimes morally difficult for the United States to support anti-communist governments in Central America?

_____

_____

_____

_____

HISTORY & GEOGRAPHY 1009: LIFEPAC TEST

80 / 100

Name _____

Date _____

Score _____

Name the continent in which each country can be found. (1 point per answer)

1. _____ Argentina
2. _____ India
3. _____ Zaire
4. _____ Mongolia
5. _____ El Salvador
6. _____ Estonia
7. _____ Portugal
8. _____ Saudi Arabia
9. _____ Mexico
10. _____ Nigeria

Choose the letter that describes the person. (1 point per answer)

11. _____ Mao Zedong		a.	Corrupt South Vietnamese leader
12. _____ Joseph Stalin		b.	U.S. president, Cuban Missile Crisis
13. _____ Ho Chi Minh		c.	Vietnamese communist leader
14. _____ Fidel Castro		d.	Last Soviet president, reformer
15. _____ Lech Walesa		e.	Chinese communist leader
16. _____ Mikhail Gorbachev		f.	Soviet leader, began Cold War
17. _____ Nikita Kruschev		g.	Military commander, Korean War
18. _____ Ngo Dinh Diem		h.	Cuban communist leader
19. _____ Douglas MacArthur		i.	Solidarity leader
20. _____ John F. Kennedy		j.	Soviet leader, Cuban Missile Crisis

Complete the statement by putting the correct letter in the blank. (1 point per answer)

21. The first artificial satellite, launched by the Soviets, was _____ .
  a. Kilimanjaro   c. Perestroika
  b. Sputnik   d. ICBM

22. Indonesia, the Philippines, and Malaysia are part of _____ .
  a. ECSC   c. NATO
  b. EEC   d. ASEAN

1

23. The world's longest river is the _____ in Africa.
 a. Nile
 b. Mississippi
 c. Niger
 d. Indus

24. The peace talks to end the Korean War stalled over the issue of _____ .
 a. repatriation of prisoners
 b. joint election of leaders
 c. troop withdrawal
 d. conquered territory

25. At the United Nations, the _____ is responsible for world peace.
 a. General Assembly
 b. Secretariat
 c. Trusteeship Council
 d. Security Council

26. When the United States learned about the missiles being installed in Cuba in 1962, the president ordered the military to _____ Cuba.
 a. invade
 b. bomb
 c. blockade
 d. threaten

27. _____ is _not_ in Central America.
 a. Honduras
 b. Nicaragua
 c. Pakistan
 d. Panama

28. The Soviets invaded _____ , on their southern border, in 1979, but Moslem rebels kept them from controlling it.
 a. Czechoslovakia
 b. Afghanistan
 c. East Germany
 d. Japan

29. _____ was a member of the Warsaw Pact.
 a. Afghanistan
 b. India
 c. France
 d. Poland

30. _____ is the second smallest continent and the only one with no deserts.
 a. Australia
 b. Europe
 c. Asia
 d. Africa

Choose the letter for the correct term. (1 point per answer)

 a. junta
 b. SALT
 c. satellites
 d. Marshall Plan
 e. Prague Spring
 f. Cultural Revolution
 g. Berlin Wall
 h. *glasnost*
 i. containment
 j. U-2 Incident

31. _____ Name given to the communist nations dominated by the Soviet Union during the Cold War.

32. _____ The United States gave money to rebuild Europe after World War II to prevent the spread of communism.

33. _____ Agreements to cut the number of nuclear weapons held by the superpowers.

34. _____ The most infamous symbol of the Cold War, prevented East Germans from reaching freedom in the West.

35. _____ A ruling military council.

36. _____ The reform movement in Czechoslovakia in 1968.

37. _____ The official American policy towards communism during the Cold War.

38. _____ An American spy plane was shot down over the Soviet Union in 1960.

39. _____ "Openness" —one of the reforms in the Soviet Union in the 1980's under the last Soviet president.

40. _____ Violent attempt to make China a classless society, led by the Red Guards.

Answer the question. (Points per question are noted in parenthesis).

41.   What was a Cold War "thaw?" (4 points)

_____

_____

_____

42.   What was the Gulf of Tonkin Resolution? (4 points)

_____

_____

_____

43.   What event triggered the breakup of the Soviet Union? (4 points)

_____

_____

_____

44.   What two European nations held the most colonies in Africa at the time of independence? (2 points)

a. _____   b. _____

45.   If you were an African leader, what would likely be your greatest problem in building a stable government for your nation? (4 points)

_____

_____

_____

46.   What were the characteristics of a nation classified as part of "Western Europe" during the Cold War? (4 points)

_____

_____

_____

Complete the following.

47.   List four nations that did not exist in 1989. (4 points)

a. _____   c. _____

b. _____   d. _____

48.   North and South America are connected at _____.
(2 points).

49.   Asia and Africa are connected at _____ (2 points).

50.   Name four nations that were officially still communist in 1995. (4 points).

a. _____   c. _____

b. _____   d. _____

51.   Name two members of NAFTA. (2 points).

a. _____   b. _____

52.   Name one "limited war" fought by the United States. (2 points)

_____

53.   Name the two main opponents, the superpowers, of the Cold War. (2 points).

     a. _____   b. _____

Write *true* **or** *false* **in each blank.** (1 point each answer).

54. _____ South American governments were frequently taken over by the military during the Cold War.

55. _____ Apartheid was the racial policy India used against its Moslem and Sikh minorities.

56. _____ Most of the former communist nations made very rapid, smooth transitions to capitalism.

57. _____ The Persian Gulf War was fought over control of Egypt.

58. _____ Most of North Africa follows the Moslem religion.

59. _____ The European Union does not include nations with constitutional monarchies.

60. _____ The Vietnam War made America more cynical and less certain of her role in the world.

61. _____ Albania and Yugoslavia set up their own communist governments after World War II.

62. _____ North and South Korea were reunited by a joint vote in 1990.

63. _____ The period of better relations between the United States and the Soviet Union in the 1970's was called *Détente*.

Select the correct letter. NOTE: one answer is used twice. (1 point each answer).

64. _____ Andes   a. Mountains, divided Europe from Asia

65. _____ Ural   b. Desert, North Africa, world's largest

66. _____ Sahara   c. River, Europe

67. _____ Congo   d. Mountain, Asia, world's tallest

68. _____ Everest   e. River, Central Africa

69. _____ Gobi   f. Mountains, Central Europe

70. _____ Superior   g. Desert, North China and Mongolia

71. _____ Danube   h. Lake, North America, world's largest

72. _____ Alps   i. Mountains, west coast of South America

73. _____ Caucasus

South American Continent

SOUTH AMERICA
THE LAND

South America is the fourth largest continent in land area covering about 6,886,000 square miles (17,835,000 square kilometers). The Pacific Ocean forms its western border and the Atlantic its eastern. It touches North America briefly at the Isthmus of Panama. The Equator runs through the northern end of the continent. South America includes the nations of Colombia, Venezuela, Guyana, Suriname, French Guiana, Ecuador, Peru, Brazil, Bolivia, Paraguay, Uruguay, Argentina, and Chile.

The Andes Mountains run in a thin line down the western side of the continent. The highest mountain is Aconcagua in Argentina at 22,834 feet. The interior of South America is a vast plain covering about 3/5 of the continent. In the east is another, much wider area of highlands broken into two sections by the Amazon River. The Amazon is the world's second longest river and has the largest drainage basin on earth. It drains about 2,700,000 sq. miles of land in South America's interior plains. Angel Falls in Venezuela has the longest drop of any waterfall in the world at 3,212 feet.

More than one third of the continent is covered with tropical rain forest, primarily in the Amazon Basin. There is growing concern about the survival of the forests as the poverty strickened population clears more and more of it for farmland. A long, thin desert area runs along the western sea coast and includes the area east of the Andes south of about the 40th parallel. Most of South America lies in the tropical zone, but due to the influence of its many mountains it has a wide variety of climates. Spanish is the region's primary language except for Brazil where the official language is Portuguese. Roman Catholicism is the dominant religion. However, evangelical Christianity is making tremendous gains.

✳ **Complete the following**

2.25   The _____ Mountains run along South America's west coast.

2.26   The world's second largest river with the largest drainage basin on earth is the

_____ .

2.27   The primary language of South America is _____ .

2.28   The tallest waterfall in the world is _____ in Venezuela.

2.29   South America is the _____ largest continent.

THE NATIONS

Northern nations. The government of Ecuador was stable from 1948 to 1960, with presidents being elected and serving their terms. A series of elected and military governments ruled from 1960-1979. In 1979, democracy was restored. Ecuador suffered a large earthquake in 1987 that left 20,000 people homeless and caused the government to temporarily stop interest payments on its foreign debt.

Colombia has had elected governments for most of its history. However, the country suffers from a great deal of unrest due to widespread poverty. From 1948-1958 the nation was convulsed by riots and fighting that killed approximately 200,000 people. *La Violencia* (the Violence) was finally ended when the two major parties agreed to govern jointly to restore the people's confidence in their leaders. More recently Colombian officials have faced violence as the nation has tried to control the powerful drug traffickers based in their country.

Venezuela was ruled by dictators prior to 1959 and elected presidents since that time. The nation has vast oil reserves and was a founding member of the Organization of Petroleum Exporting Countries (OPEC). This group was created in 1960 to help the oil producing nations gain control over the production and pricing of oil which were dominated by the United States and Europe at the time. OPEC seeks to raise the prices of oil by controlling the supply. They had a great deal of success in the 1970's. However, increased oil production from other sources and competition within OPEC has severely limited the group's effectiveness since then.

Guyana and Suriname both suffered from racial violence and government problems. Both nations have large populations of immigrants from India who were brought in as laborers when the nations were European colonies. Guyana became independent in 1966, Suriname in 1975. Guyana's economy was damaged when the government **nationalized** many of the mines and industries in the 1970's. A large portion of Suriname's population fled the country before independence causing a shortage of skilled labor. French Guiana, on the other hand, remains a territory of France and sends representatives to the French Parliament.

Central Nations. Peru's modern history has been one of unrest and government instability. Peru elected a civilian government in 1980 after twelve years of military rule. The new government faced opposition from a leftist (tending to favor communist goals) terrorist group called Shining Path. In order to combat the terrorism and economic problems President Alberto Fujimoro suspended parts of the constitution and assumed dictatorial powers in 1990.

Brazil is the industrial leader of South America. It had elected governments from 1945 to 1964, military governments from 1964-1985, and has had civilian government since that time. The military originally seized control out of fear that the government was turning towards communism. The nation has long suffered from huge inflation rates (2,148% in 1993) and a massive foreign debt. These difficulties severely hamper a potentially prosperous economy.

Bolivia has a large mining industry that dominated the government until the 1930's. The country had a constantly changing string of rulers after World War II. Most of the governments were military. A reformist government did hold power from 1951 to 1964, but was unable to control the military. Bolivia is under pressure from the United States to deal with the production of illegal drugs within its borders.

Paraguay had a military government until 1993. Civil War after World War II had led to a dictatorship under Gen. Alfredo Stroessner. He maintained political stability that encouraged investment, but made only a small portion of the people prosperous. He was overthrown in 1989 by another military officer and free elections were held four years later.

Southern nations. Chile had elected governments after World War II until 1973. In 1970 a Marxist, Salvador Allende Gossens was democratically elected as president. He began to nationalize many of the major industries and initiated land reforms. The country experienced widespread demonstrations and strikes for and against his policies. He was overthrown by a military coup in 1973. The military had the support of the United States as well as the middle and upper classes. General Augusto Pinochet Ugarte ruled the country ruthlessly until 1989 when he allowed a president to be elected. Thousands of people died under the years of harsh military rule. As of 1995, the military was still too strong to allow Pinochet to be arrested and tried for the deaths.

Argentina had a long series of civilian governments that were overthrown by military coups and then the process was repeated. One of the most enduring leaders was Juan Peron whose policies favored workers but also encouraged inflation and economic disorder. He was president in the 1950's and 1970's and his policies spawned a party of supporters, *Peronistas*. The military government that overthrew his widow ruled from 1976 to 1983. That *junta* was particularly ruthless in hunting down, torturing, and killing leftist opponents. Many people simply disappeared and have never been found. The military government captured the British Falkland Islands off the Argentine coast in 1982, but they were driven out by a British military expedition. This failure precipitated the end of military rule. Several members of the junta were later tried and convicted for their reign of terror.

Uruguay was a very prosperous democracy from World War II into the 1960's. Economic problems eventually led to terrorism and unrest. The military took over the government in 1973 and civilian rule was restored in 1985.

☞ **Match each with the correct letter.**

2.30	_____ Chile		a	Indian immigrant problems
2.31	_____ Venezuela		b.	2,148% inflation (1993)
2.32	_____ Argentina		c.	OPEC
2.33	_____ Colombia		d.	*La Violencia*
2.34	_____ Suriname		e.	Alfredo Stroessner
2.35	_____ Paraguay		f.	Salvador Allende Gossens
2.36	_____ Peru		g.	Juan Peron
2.37	_____ Brazil		h.	Shining Path

Atacama of Chile

European Continent

EUROPE

THE LAND

Europe is the smallest continent except for Australia. It covers 4,066,000 square miles (10,532,000 kilometers). The continent is bounded by the Atlantic Ocean in the north and west. The Ural Mountains, Ural River, and Caspian Sea are the eastern boundaries. A line running through the Mediterranean Sea, the Black Sea, and along the Caucasus Mountains marks the southern border.

Europe includes forty-two nations as of 1995. Twenty-four of these were free during the Cold War and were called Western Europe. Eighteen nations were under communist rule and were called Eastern Europe. These divisions were not strictly based upon geography. Nations were classified as "Western" because they were allied with the western power, the United States. These nations were also usually **capitalist democracies** located predominately on the western side of the continent. The opposite was true of the Eastern European nations.

Europe has several mountain ranges. The Alps are in southeastern France, Switzerland, northern Italy, Austria, southern Germany, and Slovenia. The Apennines run through Italy north to south. The Dinaric Alps are in Croatia, Bosnia-Herezogovina, and Yugoslavia. The Carpathian Mountains are in the Czech Republic, Slovakia, southern Poland, and touch western Russia. The Transylvanian Alps are in Romania and the Balkan Mountains are in Bulgaria. The Caucasus run between the Black and Caspian Seas in Russia. Europe's tallest peak, Mount El'brus.

(18,510 feet) is located in the Caucasus Mountains of Russia.

Europe has many important rivers. The Seine runs through Paris, France. The Rhine begins in the Alps between Austria and Switzerland and flows into Germany, at one point forming that nation's border with France. The Elbe River flows through the Czech capital of Prague and into Germany. The Danube begins in Germany and flows into Austria through its capital, Vienna. The river continues through Budapest, Hungary, into Croatia, Yugoslavia, Romania, Bulgaria, and forms the border between Romania and the Ukraine as it empties into the Black Sea. Europe's longest river, the Volga, flows southward for 2,290 miles through Russia to empty into the Caspian Sea.

Europe has mild weather for its latitude because of the warming influence of the oceans on three sides of it. The **Gulf Stream** in particular circulates warm water from the Caribbean up along Europe's coast. Some inland areas in the north do have arctic conditions. On the other hand, the Mediterranean coast has very hot, dry summers and mild winters. Europe is the only continent that has no deserts.

A wide variety of languages are spoken in Europe. The major religion is Christianity. The nations tend to be small and, historically, have changed their borders with regularity. So, the recent changes are simply part of a long-standing historic tradition.

✱ **Answer the following.**

2.38   During the Cold War, what was a "Western European nation?"

_____

_____

2.39   The Alps are located within which nations?

_____

_____

2.40   Why does Europe have mild weather?

_____

_____

_____

2.41   Describe the course of the Danube River.

_____

_____

_____

2.42   Describe the eastern border of Europe.

_____

_____

_____

2.43   What is Europe's tallest mountain and where is it located?

a. _____

b. _____

2.44   What is the longest river in Europe and where is it located?

a. _____

b. _____

THE NATIONS

Western Europe. The following is a list of the nations that were considered to be part of Western Europe. Their type of government is also noted as is whether or not they were part of the European Union in 1995. (It is noted in parentheses if only part of the country is in Europe).

Country	Type of Government	European Union
Andorra	Parliamentary democracy	no
Austria	Parliamentary democracy	yes
Belgium	Constitutional monarchy	yes
Denmark	Republic	yes
Finland	Constitutional Republic	yes
France	Republic	yes
Germany	Federal Republic	yes
Greece	Presidential parliamentary republic	yes
Iceland	Constitutional republic	no
Ireland	Parliamentary republic	yes
Italy	Republic	yes
Liechtenstein	Constitutional monarchy	no
Luxembourg	Constitutional monarchy	yes
Malta	Parliamentary democracy	no
Netherlands	Constitutional monarchy	yes
Norway	Constitutional monarchy	yes
Portugal	Parliamentary democracy	yes
San Marino	Republic	no
Spain	Constitutional monarchy	yes
Sweden	Constitutional monarchy	no
Switzerland	Federal republic	no
Turkey (part)	Republic	no
United Kingdom	Constitutional monarchy	yes
Vatican City	Papal government	no

These nations generally were allies of the United States during the Cold War and share in the victory. A few nations, such as Switzerland, were neutral. The countries were and are primarily stable democracies. Spain was ruled by a military dictator, Fransisco Franco, from 1939 until 1975. Portugal also had a military takeover in 1974, but these were exceptions in Western Europe. Most of these nations have had the same type of government since World War II. They are also industrially developed nations with some of the highest living standards in the world.

Many of these nations were ruled by elected **socialist** governments at some time during the Cold War. These governments often took control of key industries and instituted large scale social welfare systems. For example, in Great Britain (United Kingdom of Great Britain is the country's official name), Sweden, and several other nations all health care is free. Parents receive an allowance from the government for each child they have at home. Pensions are paid by the government. These benefits are very expensive and require high taxes to maintain. After World War II, Europe experienced a massive economic boom that supported these benefits.

However, tougher economic times in the 1970's, 80's, and 90's have strained government generosity. Many European governments are facing the painful problem of trying to cut back their social welfare systems. Conservative governments have come to power more frequently since the late 1970's. These leaders, such as Margaret Thatcher, Prime Minister of Great Britain (1979-1990), have sold off government owned industries and have tried to reduce government spending.

Many of the nations of Western Europe are part of the European Union. This is an organization which has slowly been uniting these nations to form a sort of United States of Europe. The members of the Union have no trade restrictions among themselves. All citizens have the right to live, work, and vote in any member nation. The Union regulates trade between the members and outside nations. The Union has agreed to establish a single currency for all of Europe, but the members were still squabbling over the details in 1995.

The Union began in 1951 as the European Coal and Steel Community (ECSC). The ECSC consisted of six nations who agreed to abolish trade barriers among themselves for coal, steel, and related products. A treaty signed in Rome in 1957 established two more organizations, the European Economic Community (EEC) and the European Atomic Energy Community (Euroatom), to allow the nations to combine their atomic resources and other aspects of their economies. These organizations were combined in 1967 as the European Community (EC). All tariffs between member nations were abolished in 1968 and common tariffs were set for trade with non-members. In 1993 the members were supposed to eliminate all border checks and other impediments to free movement in Europe, but this had not been fully implemented by 1995. The European Union officially took over from the EC in 1993 when the Maastricht Treaty took effect. This treaty further united the member nations, including the provision to create a single European currency.

The European Union has steadily grown in size since its inception. As of the beginning of 1995, there were fifteen member states. Several of the non-member nations are part of the European Free Trade Association (EFTA) which has a free trade agreement with the Union. The nations continue to seek greater European unity and cooperation.

Complete the following.

2.45   What is the common characteristic of Switzerland, Andorra, Iceland, Liechtenstein, and Sweden? _____

2.46   Name the eight nations of western Europe that still have a hereditary sovereign.

_____

_____

2.47   All European Union citizens have the right to _____
_____ in any member nation.

2.48   What is the current problem with the social welfare systems in Europe? _____

_____

_____

2.49   Name the predecessor organizations of the European Union and the year they were formed.

a. _____

b. _____

c. _____

d. _____

2.50   Western European nations generally are (economically and politically)

_____.

Eastern Europe. The following is a list of the nations that were part of Eastern Europe. Also on the chart is the date their first free, elected government took office and whether or not the nation was created after 1990. If "not yet" is written under the column for free government, it means the nation had not held multi-party, fair elections as of 1995. (It is noted in parentheses if only part of the country is in Europe).

Country	Free Government	New Country?
Albania	1992	no
Belarus	1994	yes
Bosnia and Herzegovina	1990	yes
Croatia	1990	yes
The Czech Republic	1990	yes
Estonia	1992	yes
Hungary	1990	no
Kazakhstan (part)	not yet	yes
Latvia	1990	yes
Lithuania	1992	yes
Macedonia	1990	yes
Poland	1990	no
Romania	1990	no
Russia (part)	1993	yes
Slovakia	1990	yes
Slovenia	1990	yes
Ukraine	1990	yes
Yugoslavia	1990	yes

As the chart shows, many of these nations did not exist during the Cold War. Belarus, Estonia, Kazakhstan, Latvia, Lithuania, Russia, Slovenia, and the Ukraine were part of the Soviet Union until 1991. Estonia, Latvia, and Lithuania are called the Baltic Republics. They were independent nations between the two World Wars. They were annexed by the Soviet Union in 1940 under an agreement with Nazi Germany. Bosnia & Herzegovina, Croatia, Macedonia, Slovenia, and the new Yugoslavia were part of communist Yugoslavia which split apart in 1991. The Czech Republic and Slovakia were part of Czechoslovakia. They agreed to separate peacefully in 1993. Thus, the map of Europe has changed drastically in the 1990's as it has so often before. (Find a map of pre-World War I Europe if you can and compare).

Every one of the nations of Eastern Europe is under a new system of government. They are also under a new economic system, capitalism. They face a difficult future due to significant economic, ethnic, and political problems.

The eastern nations have economies that are based upon state ownership of everything. The people were accustomed to being paid and receiving free (although low quality) medical care no matter how little or poorly they worked. The state required absolute loyalty, but it also provided for the basic needs of everyone. Moreover, the people do not know how to start businesses, make decisions, or creatively solve problems. Western nations will not buy the poor quality goods produced by former communist nations. These nations are suffering high unemployment and rising crime rates in the wake of the communist collapse.

The nations also face bitter ethnic disputes. The Czechs and Slovaks were able to settle their differences by separating peacefully. The Serbs, Croats, and Muslims in Croatia and Bosnia fought a bitter civil war that shocked the world with its brutality. Separatist groups in parts of Russia have fought with government troops. Particularly in the former Yugoslavia, ethnic hatred is a major obstacle to progress.

These nations also have unstable political systems. They have no tradition of democratic governments being voted in and out. Those who achieve power expect to keep it and exploit it. For example, the parliament of Russia in 1993 had been elected under communism. President Boris Yeltsin and the parliament came into conflict over when the parliament should face elections. When Yeltsin called for elections in 1993, members of the parliament barricaded themselves in their building and were eventually driven out by the army.

Moreover, the most experienced politicians are the former communist leaders. These people frequently dominate the new free governments. Corruption is widespread, as it was under communism, and the people have no reason to trust their government. Fifty years of misgovernment simply can not be erased quickly. The best hope for these people is the tremendous spiritual renewal that is also taking place as the Gospel is being preached. Christians praying for and working for their nations will be the salt to flavor Eastern Europe freedom.

Answer the following.

2.51   Name the European nations that were part of the former Soviet Union.

a. _____   e. _____

b. _____   f. _____

c. _____   g. _____

d. _____   h. _____

2.52   Name the nations of eastern Europe that are not new countries.

a. _____   c. _____

b. _____   d. _____

2.53   What are some of the problems facing the economies of the former communist nations?

_____

_____

2.54   What are the ethnic groups that have fought each other in the area that was communist Yugoslavia?

a. _____   c. _____

b. _____

2.55   How did the Czechs and Slovaks settle their ethnic difficulties?

_____

2.56   Name some of the political problems facing the former communist nations.

a. _____   c. _____

b. _____   d. _____

2.57   Name the Baltic Republics.

a. _____   c. _____

b. _____

2.58   What is the best hope for Eastern Europe?

_____

_____

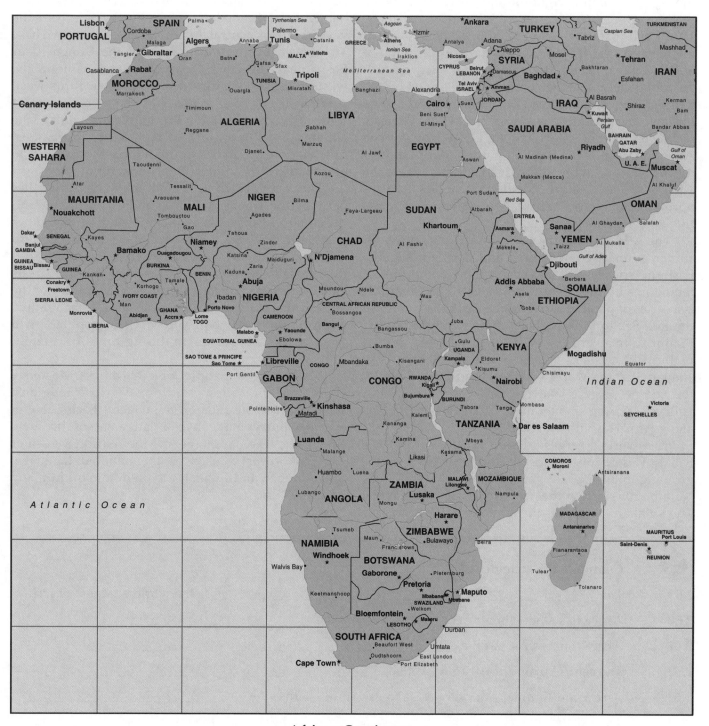

African Continent

AFRICA
THE LAND

The continent of Africa lies south of Europe with the Equator running right through its heart. It is the earth's second largest continent with an area of about 11,694,000 square miles (30,330,000 square kilometers). Africa touches Asia at the Isthmus of Suez (now split by the man-made Suez Canal). Traveling clockwise the continent is bounded by the Red Sea and Indian Ocean on its eastern side. The Indian and Atlantic Oceans meet at Africa's southwest corner, the Cape of Good Hope. The Atlantic Ocean is the western border. Africa almost touches Europe at the Straight of Gibraltar where the Atlantic Ocean meets the Mediterranean Sea, Africa's northern boundary. These boundaries encompass fifty-four nations.

The Atlas Mountains stand in Africa's northwest corner, primarily in Morocco and northern Algeria. Eastern Africa is split into deep valleys and beautiful mountains by the Great Rift System. The Great Rift is a series of parallel cracks in the earth that run from the Red Sea to Mozambique. Africa's highest peak, Mount Kilimanjaro (19,340 feet) in Tanzania, is part of the Rift System. Several lakes including Lake Tanganyika, the world's longest, and Lake Victoria, the second largest lake on earth, are also in Rift valleys. A ring of mountains also border the sea along Africa's southern coast.

The world's largest desert is in Africa. The Sahara Desert covers most of northern Africa and is growing bigger each year. Another desert, the Namib, runs along the western coast in Namibia. The Kalahari Desert sits in the center of the half circle of mountains in southern Africa. Along the southern edge of the Sahara is an area of very dry, barely habitable land called the Sahel. Further south are the vast plains of central Africa called savanna. These are broken by the rain forests of the Congo River Basin near the equator which also run along the western coast as it runs north and then turns west. Another major river is the Nile, the world's longest river, which begins in the Rift highlands south of the equator and flows <u>north</u> to the Mediterranean Sea. The Niger River arches through the western Sahel to empty into the Gulf of Guinea in Nigeria.

The majority of the land mass of Africa lies between the Tropics of Cancer and Capricorn around the equator. This makes the climate hotter than other continents. There are cooler areas in the eastern highland and the extreme south. Rainfall varies dramatically between the extremes of the rain forests and the deserts which cover more than a third of the land. Thus, Africa is a very harsh land for habitation. Many nations can barely feed their population in good years. People starve during times of drought or war.

Most of the people of Africa are Moslems, Christians, or follow traditional tribal religions. They speak thousands of languages. Each tribe, in every country may have a language of its own. Generally, the language of the nation's former colonial power is used as the national language. Thus, French and English are predominant in many African countries.

Complete the statements.

2.59   The _____ is the world's largest desert.

2.60   Africa has a hot climate because it lies across the _____ .

2.61   Africa touches Asia at the _____ .

2.62   The central plains of Africa are called _____ .

2.63   Africa and Europe come very close to each other across the _____ .

2.64   The _____ is the world's longest river.

2.65   The Congo River Basin is covered by _____ .

2.66   The Great Rift system runs where? _____

2.67   Africa's tallest mountain is _____ .

2.68   The _____ Mountains stand in Morocco and Algeria at Africa's northwest corner.

THE NATIONS

The nations of Africa were, with only one exception, all under European control at some point during their history. In fact, the nations of Africa were created by the Europeans when they divided the land up among themselves. The national boundaries do not reflect the makeup of the people. Most nations consist of many tribes or ethnic groups which have their own language, religion, and culture. The loyalty of the people and their identity is with their tribe, not their nation. Thus, tribal conflict is one of the single most divisive factors in African development.

Most of the nations of Africa were European colonies at the beginning of World War II. These were granted independence primarily in the late 1950's and 1960's. These new nations were chronically unstable. With very few exceptions, African nations were governed either by military rulers or by dictators supported by a single party during the Cold War. Many of these nations have held free, multi-party elections since 1990. This happened because the end of the Cold War cut off the support the dictators had from the two superpowers.

The following chart lists the nations of Africa, the date each became independent, and the nation it became independent from.

Country	Independence	Colonial ruler
Algeria	1962	France
Angola	1975	Portugal
Benin	1960	France
Botswana	1966	Britain
Burkina Faso	1960	France
Burundi	1962	Belgium
Cameroon	1960	France/Britain
Cape Verde	1975	Portugal
Central African Republic	1960	France
Chad	1960	France
Comoros	1975	France
Congo (Republic)	1960	France
Côte d'Ivoire	1960	France
Djibouti	1977	France
Egypt— nominally independent in 1922, but Britain held control until 1951		
Equatorial Guinea	1968	Spain
Eritrea	1993	Ethiopia
Ethiopia—retained its independence from ancient times		
Gabon	1960	France
The Gambia	1965	Britain
Ghana	1957	Britain
Guinea	1958	France
Guinea-Bissau	1974	Portugal
Kenya	1963	Britain
Lesotho	1966	Britain
Liberia	1847	United States

Libya	1952	Britain/France
Madagascar	1960	France
Malawi	1964	Britain
Mali	1960	France
Mauritania	1960	France
Mauritius	1968	Britain
Morocco	1956	France/Spain
Mozambique	1975	Portugal
Namibia	1990	South Africa
Niger	1960	France
Nigeria	1960	Britain
Rwanda	1962	Belgium
São Tomé and Príncipe	1975	Portugal
Senegal	1960	France
Seychelles	1976	Britain
Sierra Leone	1961	Britain
Somalia	1960	Britain/Italy
South Africa	1961	Britain
Sudan	1956	Britain
Swaziland	1968	Britain
Tanzania—a union of Tanganyika and Zanzibar, 1964		
Tanganyika	1961	Britain
Zanzibar	1963	Britain
Togo	1960	France
Tunisia	1956	France
Uganda	1962	Britain
Western Sahara—Spanish withdrew in 1956; occupied by Morocco		
Congo (Democratic Republic)	1960	Belgium
Zambia	1964	Britain
Zimbabwe	1965	Britain

Africa's many ethnic wars have had a devastating effect on its people. The wars often result in massacres of civilians and, worse yet, spawn famines by destroying badly needed crops. In the Sudan, for example, a civil war began in 1988 between the Moslem tribes of the north and the southern tribes which practice traditional, tribal religions or are Christian. Over 300,000 people died in 1988 due to the famine caused by the war. Over a million people starved or were killed in the Biafran War (1967-1970) that pitted the Ibo people against the Yoruba and Hausa in Nigeria. A civil war that began in Liberia in 1989 killed over 100,000 and left half the population of the country as refugees. A massacre of Tutsi people by Hutus in Rwanda resulted in an estimated 500,000 deaths in 1994. Unfortunately, the anger and distrust between the different groups can flare into fighting quickly and easily. The Rwandan massacre, for example, was set off by the death of the president (a Hutu) in an airplane accident.

Northern Africa had faced additional problems in recent years. North Africa down to the Sahel is predominately Moslem. Islam is a religion with very strict laws and rules of social behavior (such as requiring

requiring women to wear a veil and thieves to have their hands cut off). Most modern Moslem nations use western law codes and let their people choose whether or not they will follow Moslem social rules. However, a radical movement has developed in the 1980's and 90's that seeks strict enforcement of Islamic law and customs. The people in this movement are called Islamic fundamentalists. They believe that violence is an appropriate way to force Moslem governments to accept their viewpoint. This movement is led and fueled by Iran. The Iranians successfully overthrew their oppressive hereditary ruler in 1979 and established an Islamic Republic that is ruled by religion and religious authorities.

Therefore, all over northern Africa the governments have been in battles with these fundamentalists. The radicals in Egypt have specifically targeted foreigners to damage that nations lucrative tourist industry. They also have attacked and murdered Coptic Christians, an Egyptian version of Christianity that dates back to the Roman Empire. The Egyptian government has adopted a harsh policy against the radicals, arresting, imprisoning, and executing them. In Algeria, it became clear that the fundamentalists were going to win an election in 1992. The elections were canceled and the military took over the government. This type of violence and government reaction is all too common through much of North Africa.

Yet another problem plagued the nation of South Africa. South Africa was a staunch American ally during the Cold War. It also created the very discriminatory practice of **apartheid**. The majority black population was not allowed to vote, hold any of the better "white" jobs, or even live outside certain areas. Because the white rulers were anti-communist, the opposition black groups were all too often communist or communist supported. Thus, many people believed they had a choice between a discriminatory, repressive white government or a communist, repressive black government. In fact, international pressure and the end of the Cold War brought a better alternative. In 1994, under a new constitution, South Africa elected its first black president, Nelson Mandela, and the country remained surprisingly peaceful as of late 1995.

Nelson Mandela

Answer the following.

2.69   What is the dominant religion of North Africa?

_____

2.70   Apartheid was practiced in what nation?

_____

2.71   Africa's ethnic conflicts have spawned what two devastating results?

a. _____   b. _____

2.72   What types of government did most African nations have during the Cold War?

a. _____   b. _____

2.73   What two nations held the greatest number of African colonies at the time they were granted freedom?

a. _____   b. _____

2.74   What is the cause of the terrorism facing the Moslem nations of Africa?

_____

_____

2.75   Describe the problem created by the Europeans when they divided Africa.

_____

_____

_____

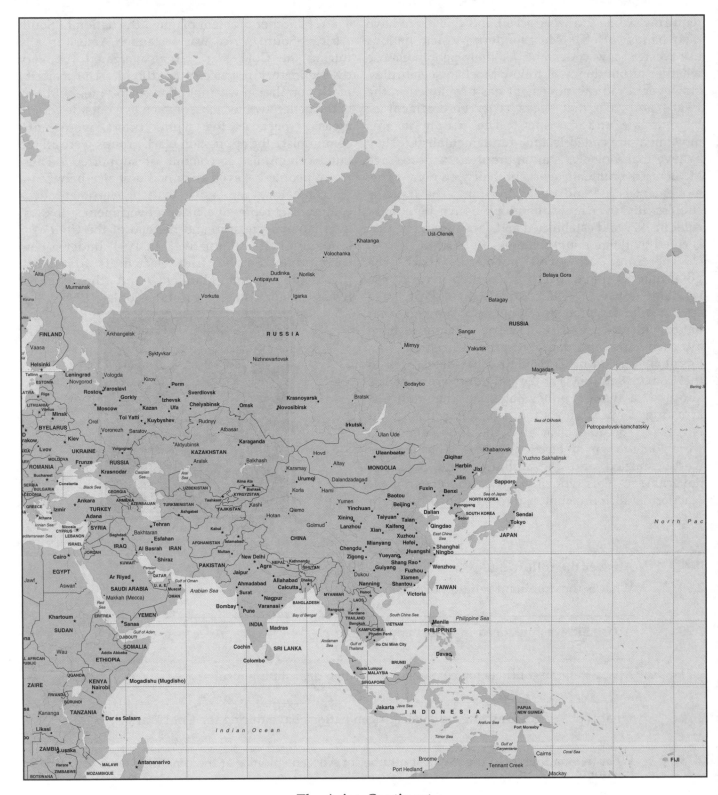

The Asian Continent

ASIA
THE LAND

The continent of Asia is located east of Europe and northeast of Africa. It is the world's largest and most populous continent. Approximately 59% of the world's people live on Asia's 16,968,000 square miles (43,947,000 square kilometers) as of 1994. the Arctic Ocean is Asia's northern boundary. Asia extends into the Pacific Ocean to the east to include the islands of Japan and the Philippines. Indonesia and Malaysia are included to the south. Otherwise, the Indian Ocean is the southern border of Asia. The continent's western border runs through the Red Sea, the Suez Canal, along the eastern Mediterranean coast, through the Black Sea, down the line of the Caucasus Mountains, through the Caspian Sea, up the Ural River and the Ural Mountains. Asia has 49 countries which this LIFEPAC divides into five regions: Middle East, Southern Asia, Southeast Asia, Far East, and the former Soviet Union.

A large portion of Asia's mountains branch out from a region known as the Pamir Knot. This region of high mountains and deep valleys is located in the area where China, Afghanistan, Pakistan, and Kyrgyzstan meet. The Himalaya Mountains run southeast of the knot through Nepal, along the border of India. The world's highest mountain, Mount Everest, at 29,028 feet, is on the border of Nepal and Tibet. The Hindu Kush Mountains run west from the Knot along the border of Afghanistan and Pakistan. Further west, the Zagros and Elburz ranges extend into Iran. The Tien Shan Mountains go northeast from the Knot along the border of China and Kyrgyzstan. The Sayan and Yablonovy Ranges run inside Russia's southern border. These flow into the Stanovoy, Verkhoyansk, and Kolyma Mountains that dominate Russia's eastern side. The Kunlun Mountains extend due east from the Knot to form the northern edge of the Plateau of Tibet; the southern edge is formed by the Himalayas.

Some of the major rivers of Asia have been the birth places of important ancient civilizations. The Tigris and Euphrates Rivers which flow through Iraq to the Persian Gulf were the home of the Sumerian, Assyrian, and Babylonian civilizations. The Indus River flows through Pakistan to the Arabian Sea. It was the birth place of the Indus Valley Civilization. The Ganges which flows through northern India and the Brahmaputra in Bangladesh are sacred to the Hindu religion. The Irrawaddy, Salween, and Mekong flow through southeast Asia. China's ancient civilization began along the Huang (Yellow) and Chang (Yangtze) Rivers that flow through the center of that nation to the East China Sea.

Asia has several deserts. The Arabian Peninsula is dominated by the Rub al Khali, a desert. The Kara Kum Desert is in Turkmenistan, while the Kyzyl Kum Desert is in neighboring Uzbekistan. The Taklimakan Desert lies north of the Tibetan Plateau. The Gobi Desert fills northern China and a large portion of Mongolia. Thus, Asia has a wide variety of land types and because of its huge size an equally wide variety of climates. It also has a wide variety of languages and religions. Islam, Hinduism, Buddhism, Shintoism, and Christianity all have significant representation in Asia.

Mount Everest

43

> **Complete the statements.**

2.76   Many of Asia's mountains branch out from the _____ on the western end of China.

2.77   The a. _____ Mountains are on the south side of the Plateau of Tibet and the b. _____ Mountains are on the north.

2.78   Asia is the _____ continent in the world in size.

2.79   The Assyrian civilization began on the a. _____ and
        b. _____ rivers.

2.80   The ancient Chinese civilization began on the a. _____ and
        b. _____ rivers.

2.81   The _____ Desert is in northern China and Mongolia.

2.82   _____ is the highest mountain on earth.

2.83   The Rub al Khali is a desert located on _____ .

THE NATIONS

The Middle East. The area of southwest Asia is generally referred to as the Middle East. It includes the nations of Yemen, Oman, Qatar, Bahrain, United Arab Emirates, Saudi Arabia, Kuwait, Israel, Jordan, Syria, Turkey, Cyprus, Iraq, Iran, and, technically, a small piece of Egypt east of the Isthmus of Suez. With the exception of Israel, which is Jewish, and part of Cyprus, which is Greek Orthodox, all the nations of this region are Moslem. Many of these nations have become extremely wealthy due to the vast reserves of petroleum in the region.

The Middle East is considered one of the "hot spots" of the world. This is because of the number of conflicts that have occurred there in recent years. Israel and Egypt fought wars in 1948, 1967, and 1973. Lebanon was racked by civil war, terrorism, Israeli and Syrian attacks through the 1970's and 80's. Dozens of foreign visitors were kidnapped and held in Lebanon, some for years, by terrorist groups. Iran's revolution in 1979 brought out a wave of official hatred towards America and Israel in that land. This resulted in an assault on the United States Embassy in Iran that same year. The embassy staff was held for over a year in violation of centuries of international law and custom. Iran and Iraq fought a war from 1980 until 1988. Iraq invaded and annexed the nation of Kuwait in 1990. The Iraqis were in turn driven out by a coalition led by the United States in February of 1991.

The end of the Cold War cut off the funds the Soviet Union gave to many of the terrorist groups in the Middle East.   The Persian Gulf War (to free Kuwait) also improved the standing of the United States in the region. Since these events, Israel has, with encouragement from the United States, entered into negotiations to give some of the land it has captured to the non-Jewish residents of Israel, the Palestinians. The process has been aided by the growing emphasis on peace since the Cold War ended.   However, radicals on both sides have engaged in acts of terrorism to stop the process, including the assassination of President Rabin of Israel by a Jew in 1995. Thus, the Middle East remains an area to watch for future conflicts.

Southern Asia. Southern Asia includes the nations of Afghanistan, Pakistan, India, Nepal, Bhutan, Bangladesh, Sri Lanka, and the Maldive Islands. Only Afghanistan became communist in this region during the Cold War. However, the Afghan people were never fully conquered by the Soviet forces sent to assist the communist government. After the Soviets left in 1988-89 the Afghans were not able to form a stable government.   Various groups continued to fight for years after the withdrawal.

South Asia is dominated by India, the second most populous nation on earth. India is often called a subcontinent because it is isolated by oceans to the sides and mountains to the north. India was a British colony until 1950.   The nations of Pakistan and Bangladesh (then East Pakistan) were created at the same time to give a homeland the Moslem minority in India.

More than twelve million people moved into or out of Pakistan (Hindus-out, Moslems-in), in the time before independence. Ethnic violence cost thousands of lives at that time and continues to be a problem. Riots after the assassination of the Prime Minister in 1984 killed thousands of Sikhs, a religious minority. Nationwide riots occurred in 1992 after Hindu radicals destroyed an important Moslem mosque. Moreover, the practices of the Hindu religion continue to hamper the nation's development by protecting troublesome animals considered sacred (such as rats) and requiring strict social divisions (caste). India remains a poor, undeveloped nation as the twentieth century ends.

Bhutan and Nepal are mountainous, isolated nations with constitutional monarchies. Both were British colonies for a time. Sri Lanka and the Maldives were also British possessions. They are located south of India in the Indian Ocean. Sri Lanka's population is divided between Buddhist Shihalese in the south and Hindu Tamil in the north. The two groups have fought frequently in the 1980's and 1990's.

Southeast Asia. This region includes the nations of Myanmar, Thailand, Laos, Vietnam, Cambodia, Malaysia, Singapore, Indonesia, Brunei, and the Philippines. Myanmar (Burma) was a British possession that suffered from frequent ethnic violence after World War II. As of 1995, it was under military rule. A large democracy movement actively opposing the junta was led by Nobel Peace Prize winner Aung San Suu Kyi.

Laos, Cambodia, and Vietnam were all part of French Indochina when World War II began. After the French failed to win control of the countries after the war, the United States fought the long, costly Vietnam War to prevent the spread of communism there. The United States also failed. By the mid–1970's all three of the nations were communist. The regime in Cambodia, the Khmer Rouge, was incredibly brutal even by communist standards. The entire population of the cities was forced to go into the jungle to clear land. Those that could not travel or work were shot. Over a million people were murdered or died of starvation. Communist Vietnam, reunited after the conquest of the North, eventually invaded Cambodia and ended the reign of the Khmer Rouge. Cambodia held free election under UN sponsorship in 1993, becoming a constitutional monarchy. Vietnam has remained officially communist but has begun pro-capitalism economic reforms since the end of the Cold War. The United States restored relations with the nation in 1995 in the hope of encouraging further reform.

Thailand, Brunei, Indonesia, Malaysia, Singapore, and the Philippines are all part of the Association of Southeast Asian Nations (ASEAN). The ASEAN was formed in 1967 and in 1976 agreed to remove all trade restrictions between the members. The region is developing quickly. Indonesia, Malaysia, and Brunei have prospered recently due to the discovery of large petroleum reserves. Singapore is a city/state that has one of the highest living standards in Asia. The governments of these nations have not been stable or democratic, however. Indonesia and Thailand were under military governments for years. The Philippines were ruled by a dictator, Ferdinand Marcos, until recently. He was elected in 1965, declared martial law in 1972, and was dramatically overthrown by a peaceful rebellion in 1986. Singapore and Brunei have only one major political party. The region's increasing prosperity may aid its stability in years to come.

Vietnam

Choose the correct letter.

2.84	_____ Afghanistan	a.	fought wars with Egypt in 1948, 1967, and 1973
2.85	_____ Kuwait	b.	battleground of the Persian Gulf War
2.86	_____ Cyprus	c.	Ferdinand Marcos ruled 1965-1986
2.87	_____ Israel	d.	part is Greek Orthodox
2.88	_____ Iran	e.	Buddhist Shihalese fight Hindu Tamil
2.89	_____ Philippines	f.	captured and held U.S. Embassy staff
2.90	_____ Sri Lanka	g.	had a communist government

Answer the following.

2.91 What was the British solution to Hindu/Moslem hatred at the time of India's independence and what resulted?

_____

_____

_____

2.92 Who were the Khmer Rouge and what did they do?

_____

_____

_____

2.93 Name the members of ASEAN.

a. _____   d. _____

b. _____   e. _____

c. _____   f. _____

Far East. The nations of China, Mongolia, Japan, Taiwan, North Korea, and South Korea comprise the Far East. China is the world's most populous nation and the last major communist country in the world. During the Cold War, China was usually preoccupied with its own problems. Thanks to Mao Zedong, the communist leader, China had plenty to worry about. Mao was a rare revolutionary who truly believed his own rhetoric. In 1958, he initialed "The Great Leap Forward." It was an attempt to transform China from an undeveloped, agricultural land into a developed, industrial nation in a few short years. People were forced to work extra long hours with no reward. Machines were run continuously without even being stopped for routine maintenance. The Great Leap failed miserably. It resulted only in hunger and economic decline.

The "Cultural Revolution" of 1966 was also initiated by Mao. He and many of his radical followers wanted to create a truly classless society. That was in conflict with more moderate views that called for trained specialists and managers to develop the economy. Mao authorized a revolution by the people to overthrow and weed out those that would try to form an upper class. Radical gangs of students called the Red Guard closed down the universities, took over several local governments, attacked businesses, and abused or killed intellectuals. The disorder became so serious that the army was activated by Mao in 1967 to end the chaos.

A power struggle followed Mao's death in 1976. The moderates won. China began to end its suicidal economic policies and establish trade relations with other nations. Farms were again given to individual owners, workers were rewarded for their productivity, and jobs were awarded on the basis of ability, not political background. China is a rapidly developing nation as of 1995. However, it is not a free nation. A pro-democracy protest in Tiananmen Square in 1989 was crushed by the army. In typical communist fashion, the Chinese government denies that any thing of the sort happened.

Japan recovered rapidly with U.S. assistance after World War II and is now one of the economic powers of the world. The former enemies now fight over their huge mutual trade. Taiwan and South Korea also experienced economic booms that have made them into developing industrial nations. North Korea remains communist and one of the most backward nations in the world. North and South Korea have never signed a peace treaty. The two nations are still officially at war. Mongolia was communist, but held free election in 1990 that the communists won. They are also beginning reforms, however.

There are two areas of potential conflict in the Far East. The first is China. China's increasingly powerful totalitarian government is hostile to any perceived threat. China claims the island of Taiwan, for example, and reacts vigorously to any sign of American support for the government there. The second area of potential conflict is North Korea. North Korea has a huge army and is increasingly isolated by the winds of political change. It has threatened to develop a nuclear bomb and used that threat to negotiate concessions from South Korea and the United States. The Far East is likely to be one focus of the next major era of world history.

The Former Soviet Union. The nations of Russia, Kazakhstan, Uzbekistan, Turkmenistan, Kyrgyzstan, Tajikistan, Azerbaijan, Armenia, and Georgia were part of the Union of Soviet Socialist Republics in 1990. These nations face problems of converting their economies and ethnic divisions. Georgia had a civil war shortly after independence and has had to deal with a separatist ethnic minority as well. Moslem Azerbaijan and Christian Armenia fought (1992-1994) over a small piece of territory populated by Armenians but located within the boundaries of Azerbaijan. Sheer survival is the main concern of these new nations.

◆   **Answer the following.**

2.94   List the Asian nations that were part of the former U.S.S.R.

a. _____   f. _____

b. _____   g. _____

c. _____   h. _____

d. _____   i. _____

e. _____

2.95   What was the purpose of the "Cultural Revolution"

_____

_____

2.96   What actually happened during the Cultural Revolution?

_____

_____

_____

2.97   What has been the economic and political situation in China since Mao Zedong's death?

_____

_____

_____

2.98   Name the two nations whose attitudes still pose a threat to peace in the Far East.

a. _____   b. _____

2.99   What was the purpose of the "Great Leap Forward?"

_____

_____

_____

2.100   As of 1995, what nations in the Far East were still officially communist?

a. _____   b. _____

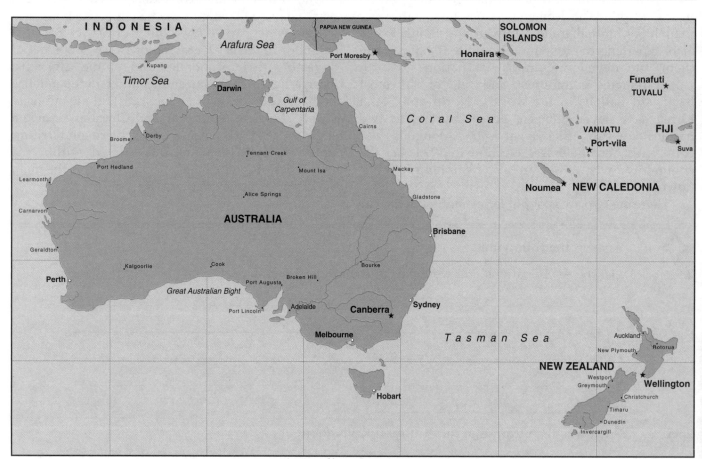

Australian Continent

THE NATIONS

Australia is both a continent and a country. It is the smallest continent, covering 2,966,150 square miles (7,682,300 square kilometers). It is an island continent in the Indian Ocean, south of Indonesia. It includes the island of Tasmania which lies south of the mainland.

The Great Dividing Range is a string of mountains that runs along Australia's east coast. The extreme southern end of this range is called the Australian Alps. The continent's highest peak, Mount Kosciusko (7,310 feet) is located there. Various deserts account for one third of Australia's land. The four major ones are the Simpson Desert in the central parts, the Great Sandy in the northwest with the Gibson and Great Victoria south of it. Few of Australia's rivers have water year round, most go dry after the rainy season. The world's largest coral reef, the Great Barrier Reef, runs along the continent's northeast coast.

Australia is a constitutional monarchy which recognizes Queen Elizabeth II of England as its head of state. The government form is a parliamentary democracy. Australia was a close ally of the United States during the Cold War. The United States, Australia, and New Zealand signed a mutual defense agreement, the ANZUS treaty, in 1951. Australia is a developed nation with large mineral wealth. It has, however, had problems with unemployment and inflation in the 1990's. English is the language of the nation and most of its people are officially Christian. There is no reason to expect such a stable nation to change much in the immediate future.

CONCLUSION

The end of the Cold War was a generous act of God. It has transformed our world. In terms of geography, twenty-two nations came into existence between 1989 and 1993. There is a movement toward democracy in many places that have never known freedom. There is a resurgence of Christianity both in the former communist countries and in many other parts of the world. Our world will always be a dangerous place as long as sinful human beings are in charge. But, by God's grace we have survived one danger that we might live to face the next.

Complete the statement.

2.101 The head of state in Australia is _____ .

2.102 Australia is the _____ continent in size.

2.103 The United States, Australia, and New Zealand signed the _____ mutual defense treaty during the Cold War.

2.104 Australia is wholly surrounded by the _____ .

2.105 The world's largest coral reef is _____ in Australia.

2.106 The four major deserts of Australia are:

a. _____   c. _____

b. _____   d. _____ .

Complete this activity.

2.107 Research any one of the newly formed nations of Asia or Europe. Do a one page report on its resources, origins, problems, and potential.

Teacher check _____
                    Initial   Date

49

Before you take this last Self Test, you may want to do one or more of these self checks.

1. _____ Read the objectives. See if you can do them.
2. _____ Restudy the material related to any objectives that you cannot do.
3. _____ Use the SQ3R study procedure to review the material:
   a. **S**can the sections,
   b. **Q**uestion yourself,
   c. **R**ead to answer your questions,
   d. **R**ecite the answers to yourself, and
   e. **R**eview areas you did not understand.
4. _____ Review all vocabulary, activities, and Self Tests, writing a correct answer for every wrong answer.

SELF TEST 2

Put in the blank the name of the continent where each feature can be found. (1 point each answer)

2.01 _____ Apennines Mountains

2.02 _____ Amazon River

2.03 _____ Gobi Desert

2.04 _____ Great Rift System

2.05 _____ Plateau of Tibet

2.06 _____ Tigris-Euphrates Rivers

2.07 _____ Great Barrier Reef

2.08 _____ Lakes Ontario and Erie

2.09 _____ Danube River

2.010 _____ Angel Falls

Complete the sentence using the words below. (1 point each answer)

Nile River   Volga River   Ural Mountains
Mount Everest   Mount Kilimanjaro   Sahara
Lake Superior   Lake Tanganyika   Andes Mountains
Congo River

2.011 The longest river in Europe is the _____.

2.012 The tallest mountain in Africa is _____.

2.013 The longest lake in the world is _____ in Africa.

2.014 The longest river in the world is the _____ in Africa.

2.015 The tallest mountain in the world is _____.

2.016 The river whose basin covers most of central Africa is the _____.

2.017 The _____ are the boundary the between Europe and Asia.

2.018 The _____ run along the west coast of South America.

2.019 The largest fresh water lake in the world is_____.

2.020 The largest desert in the world is the _____.

50

Put in the blank the name of the continent the country is in. (1 point each answer)

2.021 _____ Cambodia

2.022 _____ Suriname

2.023 _____ Honduras

2.024 _____ Gabon

2.025 _____ Slovakia

2.026 _____ Turkmenistan

2.027 _____ Greenland

2.028 _____ Australia

2.029 _____ Morocco

2.030 _____ Vatican City

Complete the sentence. (2 points each answer)

2.031 North and South America touch at the _____.

2.032 Europe and Africa nearly touch each other across the _____ at the mouth of the Mediterranean Sea.

2.033 Asia and Africa touch at the _____.

2.034 Australia is surrounded by the _____.

2.035 Cuba, Puerto Rico, the Bahamas, and Jamaica are part of the _____ Islands.

Choose the correct letter. (1 point each answer)

a. South Africa   e. Central America   h. Middle East
b. Canada   f. Venezuela   i. China
c. Latvia   g. Argentina   j. ASEAN
d. European Union

2.036 _____ Part of NAFTA, faces a separatist movement in Quebec

2.037 _____ Includes Nicaragua, Costa Rica, and El Salvador

2.038 _____ South American nation, founding member of OPEC

2.039 _____ South American military government fought the British over the Falkland Islands in 1982

2.040 _____ Successor to the ECSC and the EC, formed by the Maastricht Treaty

2.041 _____ Great Leap Forward, Cultural Revolution

2.042 _____ Baltic Republic, formerly part of the U.S.S.R.

2.043 _____ Apartheid was their policy for years, U.S. Cold War ally

2.044 _____ Includes Singapore, Malaysia, and Indonesia

2.045 _____ Predominately Moslem, site of the Persian Gulf War, part of Asia

Answer *true* **or** *false.* (1 point each answer)

2.046 _____ Most of the former communist nations are struggling against unemployment, crime, and , some, ethnic violence.

2.047 _____ The Cuban economy has been growing and prospering since the end of the Cold War.

2.048 _____ Juan Peron was an unpopular military ruler in Portugal in the 1970's.

2.049 _____ Several European nations still have monarchs.

2.050 _____ The (socialist) social welfare programs in Europe have proven to be cheap and easy to maintain.

2.051 _____ The Serbs, Croats, and Muslims of the former Yugoslavia settled their ethnic differences peacefully when communist rule ended there.

2.052 _____ Africa's ethnic wars have created massacres and famines that cost hundreds of thousands of lives in the years since independence.

2.053 _____ The Islamic fundamentalist movement in North Africa has been peaceful and supported by most of the governments.

2.054 _____ India's dominant Hindu population has come into violent conflict with Moslem and Sikh minorities since independence.

2.055 _____ The Khmer Rouge was an incredibly brutal communist party in Cambodia.

Answer the questions.

2.056   Name three of the nations of the world that were still officially communist in 1995. (2 points each answer)

a. _____   c. _____

b. _____

2.057   Using only political and historic (not biblical) information, give your opinion as to where another war will occur and why. (4 points)

_____

_____

_____

_____

_____

56 / 70

Score _____

Teacher check _____
                Initial   Date

Before taking the LIFEPAC Test, you may want to do one or more of these self checks.

1. _____ Read the objectives. See if you can do them.
2. _____ Restudy the material related to any objectives that you cannot do.
3. _____ Use the SQ3R study procedure to review the material.
4. _____ Review activities, Self Tests, and LIFEPAC vocabulary words.
5. _____ Restudy areas of weakness indicated by the last Self Test.

GLOSSARY

apartheid— Racial segregation, especially as practiced in the Republic of South Africa.

autonomy— Independence; self-government

Berlin Wall— A wall around the city of West Berlin to keep East Germans from reaching freedom there. It was dismantled in 1989, when communism collapsed in Eastern Europe.

capitalism— An economic system in which private individuals own land, factories, and other means of production

Cold War— The contest for world leadership that began after World War II between the communist nations headed primarily by the Soviet Union and the Nations of the West headed principally by the United States.

deficit— The amount of money by which a sum of money falls short.

Demilitarized Zone— A specified area free from military control; under civil instead of military control.

draft— The selection of persons for some special purpose. Men needed as soldiers are supplied to the army by draft

endemic— Something regularly found among a particular people or certain locality.

federal republic— An area which has been dominated by a single political party.

Gulf Stream— A strong, warm current that flows out of the Gulf of Mexico, north along the coast of the United States and Newfoundland, and northeast across the Atlantic toward the British Isles.

head of state— The recognized ruler in a parliamentary democracy form of government.

Intercontinental ballistic missiles— (ICBM) A ballistic missile with a range of over 5,000 miles.

Iron Curtain— An imaginary wall or dividing line, separating the Soviet Union and the nations under Soviet control or influence from the non-Communist nations after World War II.

junta— A political or military group holding power after a revolution.

Latin America— Nations of South America, Central America, Mexico, and most of the West Indies.

nationalize— To bring (industries, land, railroads, or other resources or enterprises) under the control or ownership of a nation, usually making the government responsible for their operation.

NATO— North Atlantic Treaty Organization an alliance of 14 non-Communist European and North American nations providing for joint military cooperation.

nominally— In name only; as a matter of form; in name only.

non-aligned— Not aligned politically; neutral.

parliamentary democracy— A democratic government where representatives are elected by popular vote from both the aristocracy and common citizens, and a prime minister is elected from its members.

purge— The elimination of undesired persons from a nation or party.

repatriation— To be returned to one's homeland; to restore to citizenship.

satellites—	A country that claims to be independent but is actually under the control of another, especially such a country under the control of the Soviet Union.
socialist—	A person who favors or supports socialism.
subsidies—	A grant or contribution of money, especially one made by a government in support of an undertaking or the upkeep of a thing.
superpowers—	A nation so great or strong as a power that its actions and policies greatly affect those of smaller, less powerful nations. The United States and the Soviet Union are superpowers.
thermonuclear—	Of or having to do with the fusion of atoms through very high temperature, as in the hydrogen bomb.
Third World—	Countries taking neither side in the cold war between Communist and Western nations.
Warsaw Pact—	The Soviets formed the Warsaw Pact, which claimed to be an alliance between the Soviet Union and its satellites, eventually including East Germany (created from the Soviet zone).